外国人学汉

Experiencing Chinese

英语版

Traveling in China

体验汉语®100句

旅游类

编 者 张如梅

高等教育出版社
Higher Education Press

DISC INSIDE BACK COVER

总 策 划　　刘　援

编　　者　　张如梅

英语审订　　Erin Harper

策划编辑　　徐群森

责任编辑　　金飞飞

封面设计　　彩奇风

版式设计　　高　瓦

插图选配　　陆　玲

责任校对　　金飞飞

责任绘图　　方　岚

责任印制　　韩　刚

尊敬的读者:

您好!

欢迎您选用《体验汉语100句》系列丛书。

随着全球化的发展和中国国力的不断增强,世界范围内学习汉语的人数不断增加。为满足不同国度、不同领域、不同层次汉语学习者的需求,我社策划、研发了《体验汉语100句》系列丛书。该系列丛书包括生活类、留学类、商务类、旅游类、文化类、体育类、公务类、惯用表达类等诸方面,有针对性地帮助汉语学习者快捷地掌握相关领域中最常见、最实用的中文表达。

为满足各国汉语学习者的实际需要,每册书还配有英语、日语、韩语、法语、德语、俄语、西班牙语、泰语、印尼语等九个语言版本,今后还将开发更多语种的版本。

愿本书成为您步入汉语世界的向导,成为您了解中国的桥梁,也希望您提出意见和建议。欢迎您随时与我们联系。

高等教育出版社

2007年3月

前言

《体验汉语100句》系列覆盖生活、留学、旅游、体育、文化、商务、公务、惯用表达等诸多方面，旨在有针对性地帮助汉语学习者掌握相关领域中最常见、最实用的中文表达。

本书是《体验汉语100句》系列中的旅游类。在编写时遵从了《体验汉语100句》系列共同的指导思想——注重实用性和强调交际性。本书主要针对初学汉语的旅游者编写，旨在通过本书的学习，掌握在中国旅游时最必要的100个常用句，解决在旅游交际中遇到的语言问题，是一本实用性很强的专供初学汉语的旅游者使用的语言手册。

特 点

本书以满足初学汉语旅游者的实际需求为编写目的，以旅游交际任务为编写主线，强调语料和语境的真实性和实用性，100个句子及其语境设计均来自对留学生旅游需求的访谈和调查，具有很强的实用性。

本书共有11个单元，内容涵盖了旅游中"吃、住、行、游、购、娱"六要素，能基本满足初学汉语者在旅游中的交际需求。每个单元选取的句子不仅实用，而且适用范围较广，便于旅游者使用。

本书内容简单易学。本书总词汇量为300左右，基本为甲级词，句型结构尽量使用单句，侧重句型结构的学习，避免涉及语法难点。

精美的图片、美观易检索的版式设计和悦耳的语音材料，不仅从视觉和听觉上为学习者提供了更多的语言输入方式，也增加了学习的趣味性。

附录收入了中国的节日、中国世界遗产列表、常用计量单位换算表和紧急电话号码等实用信息。

结 构

书中每个句子的学习包括常用句、对话、DIY和你知道吗四个部分。

·常用句 → 全书共收录100个常用句，每个常用句都用汉字、拼音和英语译文清楚地标明了句子的写法、读音和意义。

·对话 → 对话内容均为常用句在真实场景中的运用，以帮助学习者理解句子的意思，并学会使用和应答。

·DIY → 帮助学习者进一步灵活应用每个句子，DIY栏目提供了几个替换练习，以此加强阅读者对词汇和句型的理解和记忆，达到举一反三的效果。

·你知道吗 → 向初学汉语的旅游者补充一些旅游时必备的词汇，介绍在中国旅游的小常识，让他们对中国的人文地理有初步的了解。

编者

Foreword

Experiencing Chinese 100 series contains practical phrases pertaining to living, studying, traveling, sports, cultural communication, business communication, official communication, popular Chinese idioms and many more areas of interest. This book is *Experiencing Chinese 100 (Traveling in China)*.

This book shares the same features with others, i.e. practical and communicating. It is written especially for Chinese language beginners who like to travel in China. It provides 100 simple and essential sentences for them to solve the problems encountered during traveling in China. It's also a very practical handbook for foreign travelers.

Features

To meet the demand of Chinese beginners who like to travel in China, practicability and facility are fully emphasized in this book. The 100 sentences were chosen from the surveys of international students who traveled in China.

This book includes: food and bed, transport, sightseeing, purchase and enjoyment which can meet the demand of foreign travelers basically.

The book has very limited vocabularies, so it is very easy to learn. There are about 300 new words only and all the sentences are in simple patterns. Difficult grammar points are avoided.

Beautiful pictures and euphonic audio recording not only provide language input from vision and hearing for learners but also make the book more interesting.

The appendix includes Chinese Festivals, China World Heritage, Conversion Tables and Emergency Phone Numbers.

Structure

The book includes: Frequently Used Sentences (FUS), Conversation, DIY and Do You Know.

• **FUS:** There are a total of 100 sentences, each written in both Chinese characters and *Pinyin* with English translations and annotations.

• **Conversation:** Placing FUS in a realistic setting allows readers to better understand the meaning, usage and appropriate responses.

• **DIY:** After each sentence, DIY provides exercises for readers to practice appropriate usage.

• **Do you Know:** It introduces some necessary travel vocabulary and general knowledge when traveling in China.

Author

目录 Contents

附录 Appendix

1

请出示您的护照。
Qǐng chūshì nín de hùzhào.

Show your passport, please.

● 请出示您的护照。
Qǐng chūshì nín de hùzhào.

● 给您。
Gěi nín.

 Show your passport, please.
● Here you are.

2

请出示您的 ＿＿＿＿＿ 。
qǐng chūshì nín de

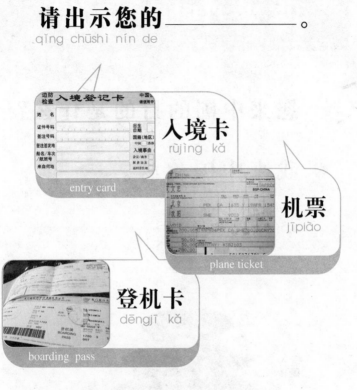

入境卡
rùjìng kǎ

entry card

机票
jīpiào

plane ticket

登机卡
dēngjī kǎ

boarding pass

女 / 男 nǚ/nán lady/man	洗手间 xǐshǒujiān rest room	收款处 shōukuǎnchù cashier
警察 jǐngchá police	问讯处 wènxùnchù information	外汇兑换 wàihuì duìhuàn exchange

3

我来中国旅游。
Wǒ lái Zhōngguó lǚyóu.

I'm coming to China for travel.

● 您来中国的目的是什么？
　Nín lái Zhōngguó de mùdì shì shénme?

● 我来中国旅游。
　Wǒ lái Zhōngguó lǚyóu.

○ What is your purpose for coming to China?
○ I'm coming to China for travel.

我来中国————————。
wǒ lái Zhōngguó

学习
xuéxí

study

工作
gōngzuò

work

经商
jīngshāng

do business

Passengers are usually asked some routine questions at customs, such as "您在中国逗留多久？(Nín zài Zhōngguó dòuliú duō jiǔ? How long will you stay?)" or "您来中国的目的是什么？(Nín lái Zhōngguó de mùdì shì shénme? What's your purpose for coming?)", etc. These questions have nothing to do with private business, and all you need is to answer them truthfully.

5

3

请打开这个箱子。
Qǐng dǎkāi zhēge xiāngzi.

Please open the suitcase.

 请打开这个箱子。
Qǐng dǎkāi zhēge xiāngzi.

 好的。
Hǎode.

Please open the suitcase.

OK.

请打开这个—————。
qǐng dǎkāi　zhège

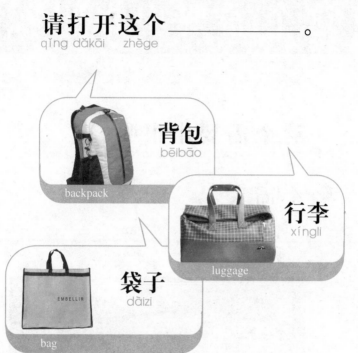

背包
bēibāo

backpack

行李
xíngli

luggage

袋子
dàizi

bag

出口	chūkǒu	exit
入口	rùkǒu	entrance
时间表	shíjiānbiǎo	timetable
抵达	dǐdá	arrival
出发	chūfā	departure

这个需要申报吗？
Zhège xūyào shēnbào ma?

Does this one need declaration?

 这个需要申报吗？
Zhège xūyào shēnbào ma?

 不需要。
Bù xūyào.

Does this one need declaration?

No.

8

需要申报吗？
xūyào shēnbào ma

相机
xiàngjī

camera

书
shū

books

光盘
guāngpán

CD

Some special articles, such as cigarettes, alcohol and perfume, should be declared. Passengers should fill in the luggage declaration form which includes the luggage number, personal items, camera, video camera, etc.

动物可以带入境吗?
Dòngwù kěyǐ dàirù jìng ma?

Can animals be brought into China?

● **动物可以带入境吗?**
　Dòngwù kěyǐ dàirù jìng ma?

● **对不起,动物不能带入境。**
　Duìbuqǐ, dòngwù bù néng dàirù jìng.

○ Can animals be brought into China?
● Sorry, animals cannot be brought into China.

10

可以带入境吗？
kěyǐ   dàirù jìng ma

水果
shuǐguǒ

fruits

肉制品
ròuzhìpǐn

meat products

植物
zhíwù

plants

DO YOU KNOW

Some articles, such as animals, plants, fruits, meat, etc, are forbidden to bring into China. They must be left at and dealt with by customs. Some articles can be kept at customs and given back to the passengers on their return, but others must be forfeited and will be confiscated by customs.

请问，在哪儿取行李?

Qǐngwèn,　　zài　　nǎr　　qǔ　　xínglì?

Excuse me, where can I get my luggage?

● 请问，在哪儿取行李?
　Qǐngwèn,　zài　nǎr　qǔ　xínglì?

● 在那儿。
　Zài　nǎr.

○ Excuse me, where can I get my luggage?
○ Over there.

请问，在哪儿————？
qǐngwèn   zài   nǎr

办理登机手续
bànlǐ   dēngjī   shǒuxù

go through the boarding procedure

办理海关手续
bànlǐ   hǎiguān shǒuxù

go through the customs procedure

托运
tuōyùn

consign

DO YOU KNOW?

Consigned luggage will arrive with your plane. You can get it in a certain area of the airport after getting off the plane. Trolley and luggage workers can offer you free service.

7

我的行李找不到了。
Wǒ de xíngli zhǎo bū dào le.

I cannot find my luggage.

● 我的行李找不到了。
Wǒ de xíngli zhǎo bū dào le.

● 别着急，再找找。
Bié zhāojí, zài zhǎozhao.

○ I cannot find my luggage.
○ Don't worry, keep looking.

14

我的 ——————— 找不到了。
wǒ de　　　　　　zhǎo bú dào le

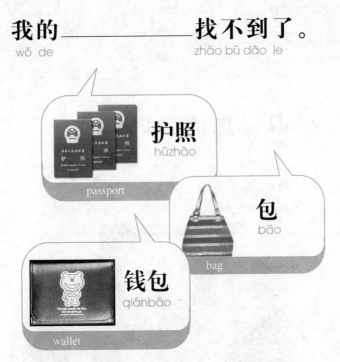

护照
hùzhào

passport

包
bāo

bag

钱包
qiánbāo

wallet

DO YOU KNOW?

　　If your consigned luggage can't be found, try to explain the situation to the airport officers in the luggage department. Show them your air ticket and luggage receipts, and they will help you. If the luggage can't be found immediately, you will be asked to fill in a lost luggage form and leave your contact details. The department will contact you as soon as they find your luggage.

谢 谢 您 的 帮 助。
Xièxie　　nín　de　bāngzhù.

Thank you for your help.

 谢 谢 您 的 帮 助。
Xièxie　nín de bāngzhù.

 不 客 气。
Bú　kēqi.

Thank you for your help.

You are welcome.

谢谢您的————————。
xièxie nín de

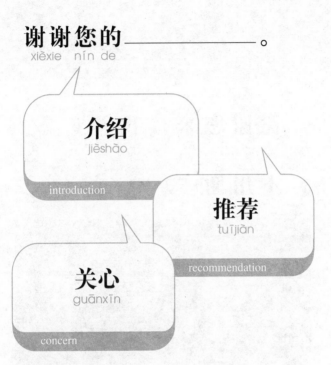

介绍
jièshǎo

introduction

推荐
tuījiàn

recommendation

关心
guānxīn

concern

You always encounter something unexpected when you go out. One of the best solutions is to know how to ask others for help. Warmhearted Chinese people are always willing to help foreign visitors. By introducing or recommending something special in their own land, they show their hospitality.

谢 谢 您 来 接 我 。

Xièxie nín lái jiē wǒ.

Thank you for picking me up.

谢谢您来接我。
Xièxie nín lái jiē wǒ.

不用谢。
Búyòng xiè.

Thank you for picking me up.

You are welcome.

谢谢您来————————我。
xièxie nín lái　　　　　　wǒ

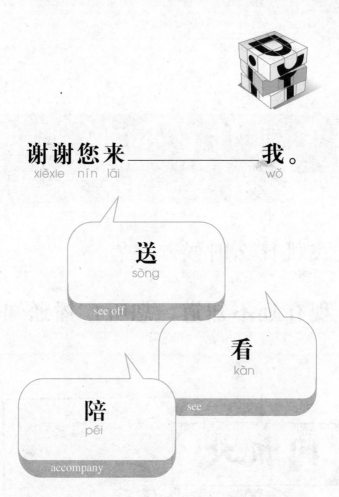

送
sòng
see off

看
kàn
see

陪
péi
accompany

Passengers traveling with a travel agency are usually met at the airport by a tour guide who has written the passengers' names on a board, and waits at the exit holding it. Pay attention to the board if you are traveling with a travel agency.

飞机什么时候起飞?
Fēijī shénme shíhou qǐfēi?

When will the plane take off?

飞机什么时候起飞?
Fēijī shénme shíhou qǐfēi?

现在还不知道,您听广播通知吧。
Xiànzài hái bù zhīdào, nín tīng guǎngbō tōngzhī ba.

When will the plane take off?

We don't know yet. Please listen to the broadcast.

飞机什么时候——————?
fēijī shénme shíhou

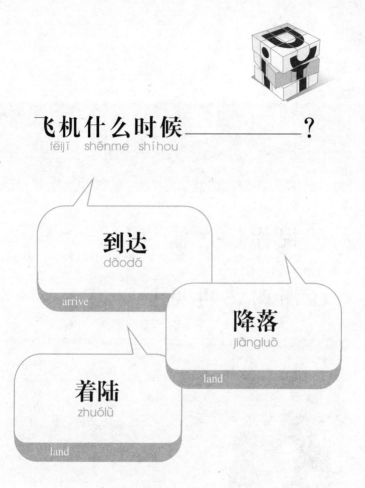

到达
dǎodá

arrive

降落
jiàngluǒ

land

着陆
zhuólù

land

Mandarin is spoken throughout China, and English is becoming more and more common. In areas frequently visited by tourists, you won't have any problems using English. But it is helpful to learn simple survival Chinese as presented in this book.

祝你旅途愉快！
Zhù nǐ lǚtú yúkuài!

Wish you a pleasant trip!

● 祝你旅途愉快！
Zhù nǐ lǚtú yúkuài!

● 谢谢，再见！
Xièxie, zàijiàn!

○ Wish you a pleasant trip!
● Thank you. Good-bye!

祝 你————————!
zhù nǐ

一路平安
yílù píng'ān

good journey

心情愉快
xīnqíng yúkuài

good humor

好运
hǎoyùn

good luck

It is common to experience some small discomfort when you travel by plane. The following are some tricks for these indispositions.

- **Ear pain, ringing**: Chew gum, or put wet cotton balls in your ears. It will help to relieve the pain.
- **Sore throat**: Drink lots of water. Mint and other throat lozenges will also be very useful.
- **Airsickness**: As with carsickness and seasickness, medicine can be very useful. Ginger is also very effective in treating airsickness.

请问，机场大巴在哪儿？

Qǐngwèn, jīchǎng dàbā zài nǎr?

Excuse me, where is the airport bus station?

● 请问，机场大巴在哪儿？

　Qǐngwèn, jīchǎng dàbā zài nǎr?

● 往前走，在门口往左拐就看见了。

　Wǎngqián zǒu, zài ménkǒu wǎng zuǒ guǎi jiù kànjiàn le.

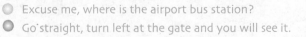

○ Excuse me, where is the airport bus station?

○ Go straight, turn left at the gate and you will see it.

请问，————————在哪儿？
qǐngwèn　　　　　　　　　zài　 nǎr

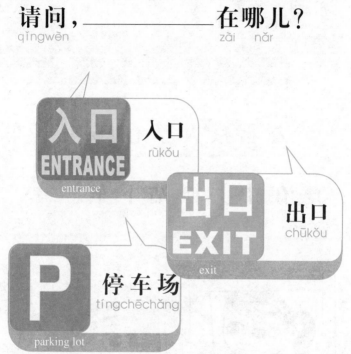

入口
rùkǒu
entrance

出口
chūkǒu
exit

停车场
tíngchēchǎng
parking lot

The airport bus can take you to different areas of downtown. It is very convenient and the price is reasonable. Passengers can inquire the routes and prices from internet in advance.

13

去北京大学在哪儿下车？
Qù Běijīng Dàxué zài nǎr xiàchē?

Where do I get off to go to Peking University?

- 去北京大学在哪儿下车？
  Qù Běijīng Dàxué zài nǎr xiàchē?

- 在中关园站下车。
  Zài Zhōngguānyuán zhàn xiàchē.

- Where do I get off to go to Peking University?
- At Zhongguanyuan stop.

26

去 —————— 在哪儿下车？
qù　　　　　　　　zài　nǎr　xiàchē

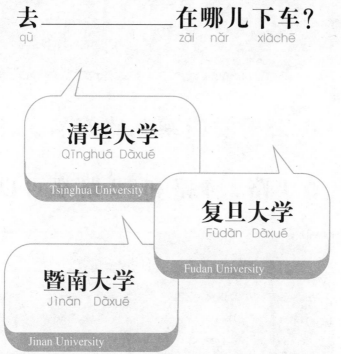

清华大学
Qīnghuá Dàxué

Tsinghua University

复旦大学
Fùdàn Dàxué

Fudan University

暨南大学
Jìnán Dàxué

Jinan University

DO YOU KNOW

The hot line of Beijing Guide is 1605106 and 16885106. You can also send a message by mobile phone to 9555156 to ask directions. Foreign language service is available for Beijing Guide and costs one yuan per minute. The Civil Administration Department is currently working on setting up a China Guide system.

去天安门乘几路车？
Qù Tiān'ānmén chéng jǐ lù chē?

Which bus do I take to go to Tian'anmen Square?

● 去天安门乘几路车？
Qù Tiān'ānmén chéng jǐ lù chē?

● 1路、4路和52路都可以。
Yī lù, sì lù hé wǔshí'èr lù dōu kěyǐ.

○ Which bus do I take to go to Tian'anmen Square?

○ No.1, No.4, and No.52 are all available.

去 —————— 乘几路车？
qù　　　　　　　chéng jǐ lù chē

故宫
Gùgōng

Forbidden City

天坛
Tiāntán

Temple of Heaven

雍和宫
Yōnghégōng

Lama Temple

DO YOU KNOW?

Apart from post office, mail service is also available in some hotels. When mailing a letter, make sure to use a standard envelope, fill in the postal code, and attach the right amount of stamps. Express mail service is available at most post offices and express mail companies.

到颐和园还有几站？
Dào　　　Yíhéyuán　　　hái　yǒu　jǐ　zhàn?

How many stops are there to get to the Summer Palace?

到 颐 和 园 还 有 几 站？
Dào　Yíhéyuán　hái　yǒu　jǐ　zhàn?

还 有 三 站。
Hái　yǒu　sān　zhàn.

How many stops are there to get to the Summer Palace?
There are three stops.

到—————还有几站？
dào　　　　hái yǒu jǐ zhàn

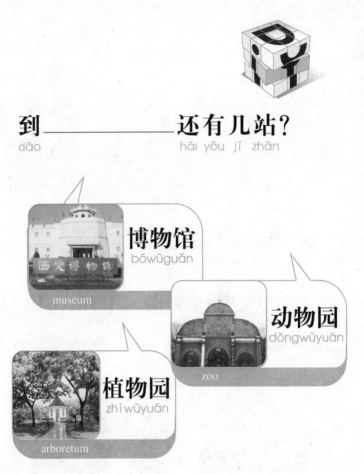

博物馆
bówùguǎn

museum

动物园
dòngwùyuán

zoo

植物园
zhíwùyuán

arboretum

Now many buses use bus cards or ticket self-service instead of bus conductor. Passengers get on the bus through the front door and swipe their cards. If the bus is very crowded, you'd better get ready two stops before you get off.

去友谊宾馆怎么走？
Qù Yǒuyì Bīnguǎn zěnme zǒu?

How do I get to the Friendship Hotel?

● 去友谊宾馆怎么走？
　Qù　Yǒuyì Bīnguǎn zěnme　zǒu?

● 一直走，到第二个路口往右拐。
　Yìzhí　zǒu,　dào　dì'èr　gè　lùkǒu wǎng yòu guǎi.

○ How do I get to the Friendship Hotel?
● Go straight, and turn right at the second corner.

去 ————— 怎么走？
qù   zěnme   zǒu

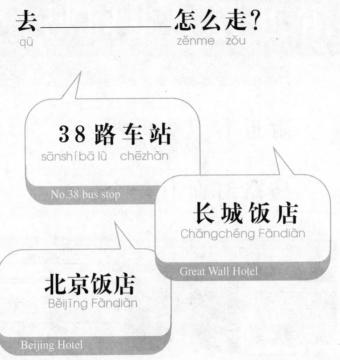

38路车站
sānshíbā lù   chēzhàn

No.38 bus stop

长城饭店
Chángchéng Fàndiàn

Great Wall Hotel

北京饭店
Běijīng Fàndiàn

Beijing Hotel

When asking directions, ask the helper to give you directions using location words like "left, right, ahead and behind" instead of "east, west, south and north" in case you are not familiar with these geography locations.

附 近 有 卫 生 间 吗 ?
Fùjìn yǒu wèishēngjiān ma?

Is there a toilet nearby?

● 附近有卫生间吗？
Fùjìn yǒu wèishēngjiān ma?

● 马路对面有一个。
Mǎlù duìmiàn yǒu yí gè.

○ Is there a toilet nearby?
○ Yes, there is one on the other side of the street.

34

附近有————吗？
fùjìn yǒu   ma

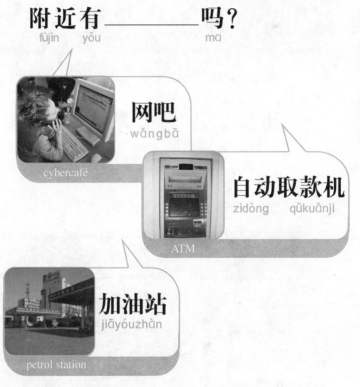

网吧
wǎngbā

cybercafé

自动取款机
zìdòng qǔkuǎnjī

ATM

加油站
jiāyóuzhàn

petrol station

DO YOU KNOW

- There are toilets for tourists at most scenic sites, but some of them charge 2–5 jiao.
- There are free toilets in shopping centers and supermarkets.
- There are toilets in subway stations and train stations.

师傅，去火车站大概多少钱?

Shīfu, qù huǒchēzhàn dàgài duōshao qián?

Master, how much does it cost to go to the train station?

● **师傅，去火车站大概多少钱?**
　　Shīfu, qù huǒchēzhàn dàgài duōshao qián?

● **50块。**
　　Wǔshí kuǎi.

○ Master, how much does it cost to go to the train station?

○ 50 yuan.

师傅，去——大概多少钱？
shīfu　　qù　　　　　dàgài　duōshao qiǎn

长城
Chángchéng

the Great Wall

机场
jīchǎng

airport

王府井
Wángfǔjǐng

Wangfujing

"Shīfu (master)" is a general term for those who serve you. It is advisable to ask the price before you decide to go somewhere. The starting price of a taxi is about 10 yuan and then 2 yuan for per kilometer. An additional 20% price will be added between 11 pm. and 5 am.

我去圆明园。

Wǒ qù Yuánmíngyuán.

I am going to Yuanmingyuan.

 您去哪儿？

Nín qù nǎr?

 我去圆明园。

Wǒ qù Yuánmíngyuán.

Where are you going?

I am going to Yuanmingyuan.

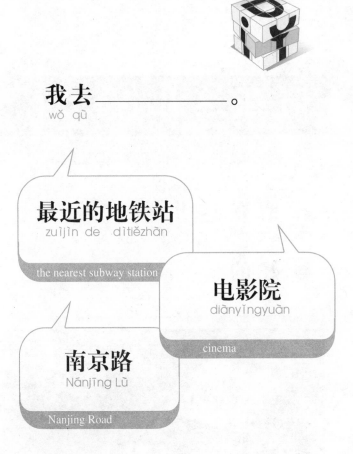

我去 ———————。
wǒ qù

最近的地铁站
zuìjìn de dìtiězhàn

the nearest subway station

电影院
diànyǐngyuàn

cinema

南京路
Nánjīng Lù

Nanjing Road

When taking a taxi, it's best to tell the driver the exact address, such as the name of the street and the door number. For the big place, give him/her a more detailed location, for example, the east gate of Peking University, otherwise you may lose your way.

39

请 在 这 儿 停 一 下 。
Qǐng zài zhèr tíng yíxià.

Please stop here for a while.

 请 在 这 儿 停 一 下 。
Qǐng zài zhèr tíng yíxià.

好 的 。
Hǎode.

Please stop here for a while.

OK.

请————————。
qǐng

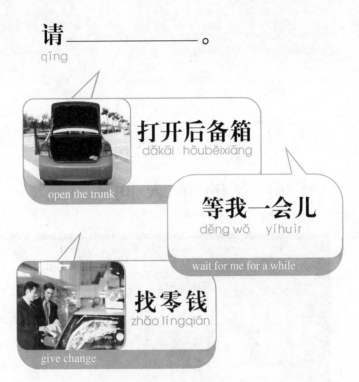

打开后备箱
dǎkāi hòubèixiāng

open the trunk

等我一会儿
děng wǒ yíhuìr

wait for me for a while

找零钱
zhǎo língqián

give change

In a taxi, if you want to stop temporarily, you should first ask if taxis can stop at that location. The meter is on during short stops, so the shorter, the better.

41

有空房间吗？
Yǒu kōng fángjiān ma?

Are there any rooms available?

● 有空房间吗？
Yǒu kōng fángjiān ma?

● 有空的单人间。
Yǒu kōng de dānrénjiān.

○ Are there any rooms available?
○ Yes, a single room is available.

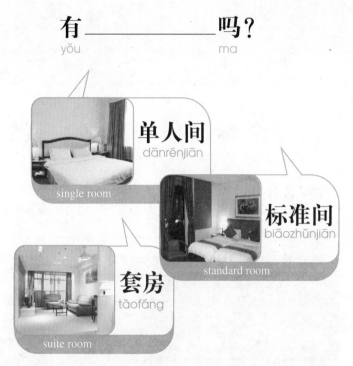

有 ——————— 吗？
yǒu   ma

单人间
dānrénjiān
single room

标准间
biāozhǔnjiān
standard room

套房
tāofáng
suite room

DO YOU KNOW

- **Single room**: 16−20 square meters with a bathroom and other amenities, including one bed.
- **Standard**: two beds or one double bed with a bathroom and other amenities. It is for two persons or a couple and is the choice of most travel groups.
- **Luxury room**: two beds or one double bed with a bathroom and other amenities. It has more amenities and services and is more expensive than single and standard rooms.

一个标准间一天多少钱？

Yí gè biāozhǔnjiān yì tiān duōshao qián?

How much is a standard room per day?

● 一个标准间一天多少钱？

Yí gè biāozhǔnjiān yì tiān duōshao qián?

● 360 块。

Sānbǎi liùshí kuài.

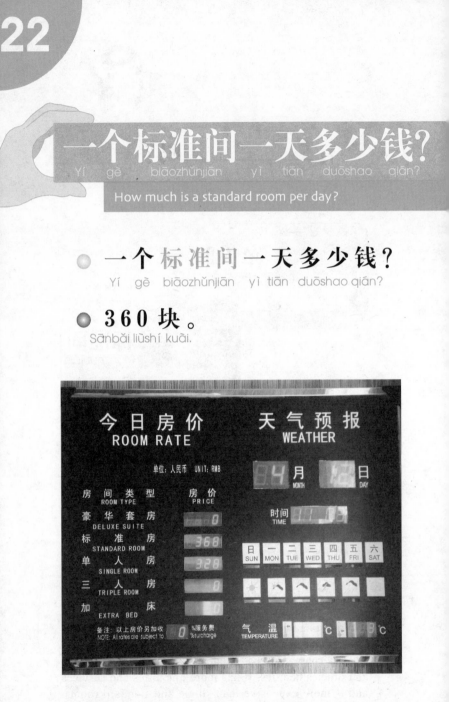

今日房价 ROOM RATE　　天气预报 WEATHER

单位：人民币 UNIT: RMB

房间类型 ROOM TYPE	房价 PRICE
豪华套房 DELUXE SUITE	0
标准房 STANDARD ROOM	368
单人房 SINGLE ROOM	328
三人房 TRIPLE ROOM	0
加床 EXTRA BED	0

备注：以上房价另加收 0 %服务费
NOTE: All rates are subject to %surcharge

How much is a standard room per day?

360 yuan.

一个 ————— 一天多少钱？
yí gè   yì tiān duōshao qián

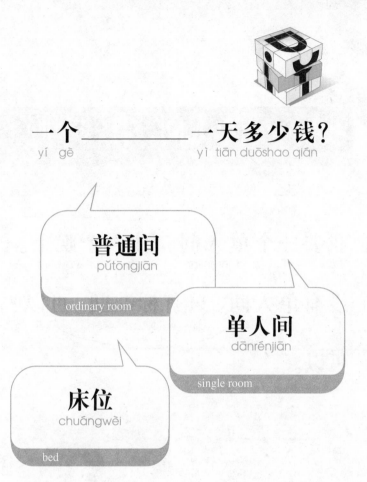

普通间
pǔtōngjiān

ordinary room

单人间
dānrénjiān

single room

床位
chuángwèi

bed

DO YOU KNOW ?

The quoted price is not the guaranteed price in most hotels. Especially in busy season, the room price changes even daily, so it is advisable to ask the room price at the reception desk of the hotel.

我要一个单人间，住一个晚上。
Wǒ yào yí gè dānrénjiān, zhù yí gè wǎnshang.

I want a single room for one night.

● 我要一个单人间，住一个晚上。
Wǒ yào yí gè dānrénjiān, zhù yí gè wǎnshang.

● 没有单人间，只有标准间，可以吗？
Méiyǒu dānrénjiān, zhǐyǒu biāozhǔnjiān, kěyǐ ma?

● 可以。
Kěyǐ.

标准间——XX
双人间——XX
——XX

○ I want a single room for one night.
● There are no single rooms, only standard ones. Will that work?
○ Yes.

我要一个单人间，住————。
wǒ yào yí gè dānrénjiān zhù

两天
liǎng tiān
two days

一个星期
yí gè xīngqī
a week

半年
bànnián
half a year

When checking in, keep important and valuable articles at the reception desk so that you can go out feeling relaxed and carefree. In some big hotels, there is a safe rental service.

房价打折吗？

Fángjià dǎzhé ma?

Is there any discount on the room price?

○ 房价打折吗？
　Fángjià dǎzhé ma?

● 打折。
　Dǎzhé.

○ 打几折？
　Dǎ jǐ zhé?

○ 打八折。
　Dǎ bā zhé.

○ Is there any discount on the room price?
● Yes.
○ How much is the discount?
○ 20% off.

————————打折吗？
dǎzhé ma

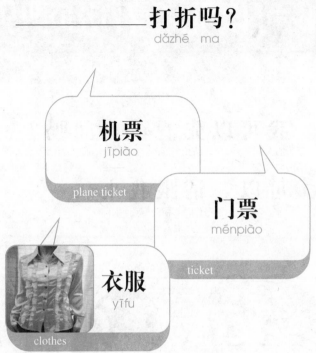

机票
jīpiào

plane ticket

门票
ménpiào

ticket

衣服
yīfu

clothes

DO YOU KNOW ?

Usually there is a discount at hotels and other businesses, especially in the slow season. In Chinese, discount is expressed from 1−9 zhé, which means 90%−10% discount. 8.8 zhé is often used because 8 has the same partial tone as fā, which means making a lot of money. 8.8 zhé equals a 12% discount.

我可以先看看房间吗？
Wǒ　kěyǐ　　xiān　kànkan　fángjiān　ma?

Can I have a look at the room first?

● **我可以先看看房间吗？**
Wǒ　kěyǐ　xiān　kànkan　fángjiān　ma?

● **可以。请跟我来。**
Kěyǐ.　　Qǐng gēn　wǒ　lái.

○ Can I have a look at the room first?
● Yes, please follow me.

我可以先＿＿＿＿＿吗？
wǒ　kěyǐ　xiān　　　　　　　ma

试试热水
shìshi　rèshuǐ

try the hot water

听听音乐
tīngting　yīnyuè

listen to music for a while

休息一下
xiūxi　yíxià

rest for a while

Check-in time: from 14: 00 p.m.
Check-out time: before 12.00 p.m.
Check-in and check-out time is subject to the management of the specific hotel. It is advisable to contact the hotel if you need earlier check-in or later check-out. Early check-in or late check-out sometimes result in an extra charge.

26

我预订了一个房间。

Wǒ yùdìng le yí gè fángjiān.

I have reserved a room.

● 我叫大卫，三天前我预订了一个房间。
Wǒ jiào Dàwèi, sān tiān qián wǒ yùdìng le yí gè fángjiān.

● 请稍等。对，您预订了一个单人间。
Qǐng shāoděng. Duì, nín yùdìng le yí gè dānrénjiān.

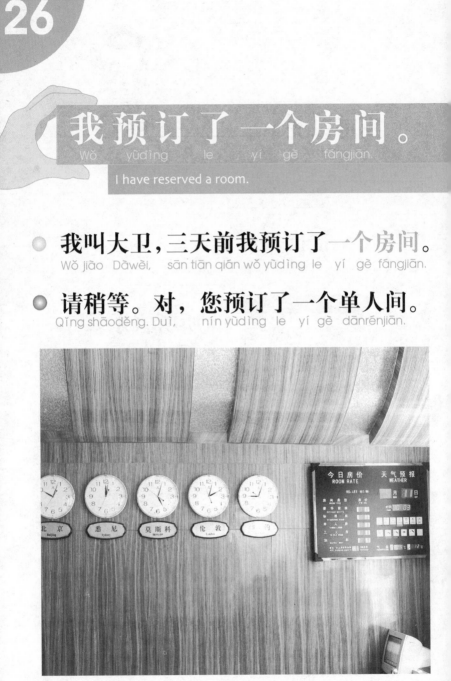

● My name is David. I reserved a room three days ago.

● Just a minute. Yes, you reserved a single room.

我预订了————————。
wǒ yùdìng le

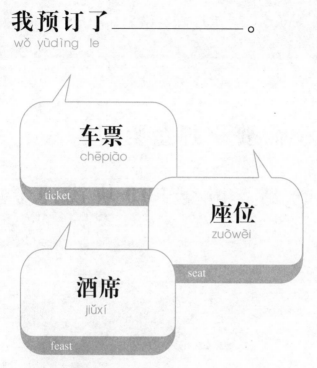

车票
chēpiào

ticket

座位
zuòwèi

seat

酒席
jiǔxí

feast

Reservation is necessary, especially in busy season. Usually you can make a reservation by phone at least three days in advance. The reservation number is 800-820-6666(free). Internet reservation is also available through http://www.ctrip.com.

27

需要交押金吗？
Xūyào jiāo yājīn ma?

Shall I place a deposit?

● 需要交押金吗？
Xūyào jiāo yājīn ma?

● 要，请交100块钱押金。
Yào, qǐng jiāo yìbǎi kuài qián yājīn.

○ Shall I place a deposit?
● Yes, it's 100 yuan for a deposit.

需要 _____ 吗?
xūyào   ma

填表
tiánbiǎo

fill in the form

签字
qiānzì

sign name

开发票
kāi fāpiào

issue an invoice

You have to place a deposit in most hotels so that you can get the room card or the key. The deposit will be returned when you settle the account before leaving. It is not necessary to pay tips in the hotel.

28

请 收 好 押 金 收 据 。

Qǐng shōuhǎo yājīn shōujù.

Please hold on to the deposit receipt.

● 请收好押金收据。
Qǐng shōuhǎo yājīn shōujù.

● 好的， 谢谢。
Hǎode, xièxie.

○ Please hold on to the deposit receipt.
○ OK, thank you.

请收好————。
qǐng shōuhǎo

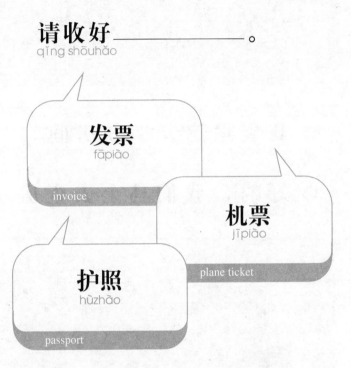

发票
fāpiào

invoice

机票
jīpiào

plane ticket

护照
hùzhào

passport

Deposit is usually required for the room card and facilities. When you check out, you can get the deposit back with your receipt only after the room is checked to see that nothing is broken.

29

我要退房，309房间。
Wǒ yào tuìfáng, sānlíngjiǔ fángjiān.

I want to check out, room 309.

● 我要退房，309房间。
Wǒ yào tuìfáng, sānlíngjiǔ fángjiān.

● 好的，我们马上去查房。
Hǎode, wǒmen mǎshàng qù cháfáng.

● I want to check out, room 309.
● OK, we will go there for checking.

58

我要————————。
wǒ yào

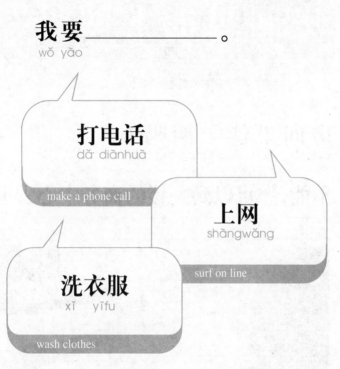

打电话
dǎ diànhuà

make a phone call

上网
shàngwǎng

surf on line

洗衣服
xǐ yīfu

wash clothes

Please check your own belongings before you check out so you don't lose anything. Check out before 12pm, because you will be charged an additional half of the room price if you check out after 12pm.

59

30

房间里能上网吗？
Fángjiān lǐ néng shàngwǎng ma?

Is internet available in the room?

● 房间里能上网吗？
Fángjiān lǐ néng shàngwǎng ma?

● 不能，您可以到一楼的商务中心去上网。
Bù néng, nín kěyǐ dào yī lóu de shāngwù zhōngxīn qù shàngwǎng.

● Is internet available in the room?
● No, you can use the internet in the business center on the first floor.

房间里＿＿＿＿＿吗？
fángjiān li   ma

能打国际长途电话
néng dǎ guójì chángtú diànhuà

can make an international call

能看CNN
néng kàn CNN

can receive CNN

允许抽烟
yǔnxǔ chōuyān

can smoke

Internet is available in most hotels, but it is not free. Internet use costs about 2－5 yuan per hour. You can make international calls in the hotel, but it is more expensive than making them from a public telephone. Buy an IP card or IC card to make phone calls. Telephone cards can be bought in hotels, train stations or any small shop.

31

帮我换一个枕头，好吗？
Bāng wǒ huàn yí gè zhěntou, hǎo ma?

Please change the pillow for me, Ok?

● 帮我换一个枕头，好吗？
Bāng wǒ huàn yí gè zhěntou, hǎo ma?

● 好的，马上拿过来。
Hǎode, mǎshàng ná guòlái.

Please change the pillow for me, OK?

OK, I will have it done as soon as possible.

帮我换————，好吗？
bāng wǒ huàn　　　hǎo ma

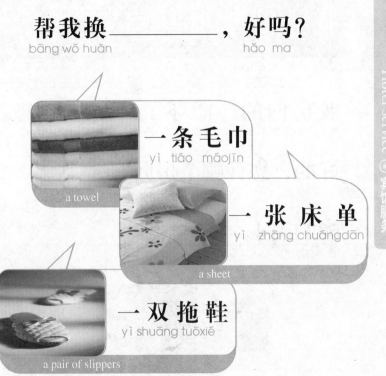

一条毛巾
yì tiáo máojīn

a towel

一张床单
yì zhāng chuángdān

a sheet

一双拖鞋
yì shuāng tuōxié

a pair of slippers

DO YOU KNOW

Hotels in China are star-rated by international standards, from one star to five stars. A 3-star hotel includes private bathroom with tub, TV, central air-conditioning, telephone, restaurant meals around-the-clock, post office, shop, sauna, fitness center, business center and beauty parlor.

我房间的马桶坏了，请修一修。

Wǒ fángjiān de mǎtǒng huài le, qǐng xiū yi xiū.

The toilet in my room is broken. Please repair it.

我房间的马桶坏了，请修一修。
Wǒ fángjiān de mǎtǒng huài le, qǐng xiū yi xiū.

好的，您住哪个房间？
Hǎode, nín zhù nǎge fángjiān?

502 房间。
Wǔlíng'èr fángjiān.

The toilet in my room is broken. Please repair it.

OK. Which room are you in?

Room 502.

我房间的————坏了，请修一修。
wǒ fángjiān de　　　　　 huài le 　 qǐng xiū yi xiū

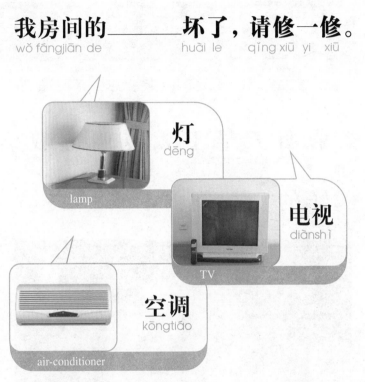

灯
dēng

lamp

电视
diànshì

TV

空调
kōngtiáo

air-conditioner

Electricity in China is 220V, 50 cycle, AC. Both two-pin sockets and some three-pin sockets are in use. Most hotels have a socket in the bathroom for both 110V and 220V, as well as built-in converters for shavers, hair dryers, etc. Outside the bathroom, only 220V sockets are provided, so a converter will be required to change the voltage from 220V to 110V. Most hotels will have adapters, but it is always wise to be prepared if you have some piece of electrical equipments which you need to use.

33

请明天早上六点叫醒我。

Qǐng míngtiān zǎoshang liù diǎn jiàoxǐng wǒ.

Please give me a wake-up call at 6 am tomorrow.

● 请 明 天 早 上 六 点 叫 醒 我 。

Qǐng míngtiān zǎoshang liù diǎn jiàoxǐng wǒ.

● 好 的 。

Hǎode.

○ Please give me a wake-up call at 6 am tomorrow.

○ OK.

请明天早上 ——— 叫醒我。
qǐng míngtiān zǎoshang　　　　jiàoxǐng wǒ

七点
qī diǎn

7 am

八点
bā diǎn

8 am

六点半
liù diǎn bàn

6:30 am

Wake-up calls are free in most hotels. The person on duty will wake up the guests by calling. Some big hotels use an automatic system for wake-up calls, so guests who need a wake-up call can set the time and room number by themselves, or can ask the receptionist on duty to set it. The automatic system will work through the telephone the next morning.

34

请打扫一下我的房间。

Qǐng dǎsǎo yíxià wǒ de fángjiān.

Please clean my room.

请打扫一下我的房间。
Qǐng dǎsǎo yíxià wǒ de fángjiān.

好的，我马上打扫。
Hǎode, wǒ mǎshàng dǎsǎo.

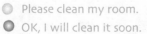
Please clean my room.

OK, I will clean it soon.

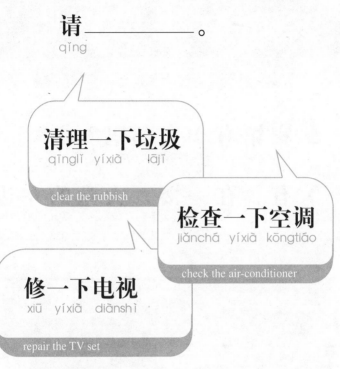

请 ——————。
qǐng

清理一下垃圾
qīnglǐ yíxià lājī

clear the rubbish

检查一下空调
jiǎnchá yíxià kōngtiáo

check the air-conditioner

修一下电视
xiū yíxià diànshì

repair the TV set

The tap water is potable only in a limited number of luxury hotels, so make sure to ask the hotel manager if it is safe to drink the tap water. All guest rooms in Chinese hotels are equipped with thermos bottles filled with boiled water. Bottled mineral water is also popular in China nowadays.

35

宾馆有小卖部吗？
Bīnguǎn yǒu xiǎomàibù ma?

Is there a buffet in the hotel?

○ 宾馆有小卖部吗？
Bīnguǎn yǒu xiǎomàibù ma?

● 有，在一楼，大堂的左边。
Yǒu, zài yī lóu, dàtáng de zuǒbian.

○ Is there a buffet in the hotel?

● Yes, on the first floor, the left side of the lobby.

宾馆有————吗？
bīnguǎn yǒu ma

游泳池
yóuyǒngchí
swimming pool

健身房
jiānshēnfáng
gym

咖啡厅
kāfēitīng
café

DO YOU KNOW?

There are some home-stays in scenic sites that are run by local people with extra rooms in their homes. Home-stays are simply equipped but lower priced. You can feel the home atmosphere staying with local people and really know their lifestyles, which can be a meaningful addition for your travels.

36

餐厅几点营业？
Cāntīng jǐ diǎn yíngyè?

When is the service time for the restaurant?

● 餐厅几点营业？
Cāntīng jǐ diǎn yíngyè?

● 从早上6点到晚上12点。
Cóng zǎoshang liù diǎn dào wǎnshang shí'èr diǎn.

○ When is the service time for the restaurant?
○ From 6 am to 12 midnight.

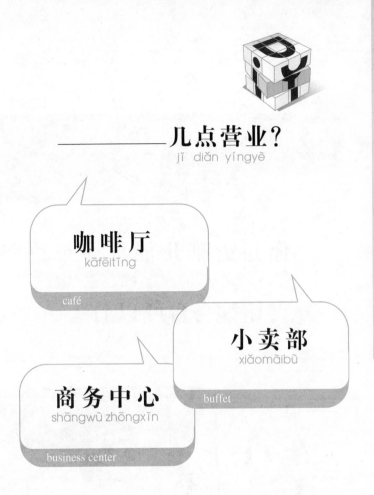

几点营业？
jǐ diǎn yíngyè

咖啡厅
kāfēitīng
café

小卖部
xiǎomǎibù
buffet

商务中心
shāngwù zhōngxīn
business center

Usually there are booklets introducing the services of the hotel in the lobby. Take one when you register so that you can learn about service offerings of the hotel in detail.

37

你知道哪儿能订火车票吗?

Nǐ zhīdào nǎr néng dìng huǒchēpiào ma?

Do you know where I can reserve a train ticket?

 你知道哪儿能订火车票吗?

Nǐ zhīdào nǎr néng dìng huǒchēpiào ma?

宾馆服务台可以订。

Bīnguǎn fúwùtái kěyǐ dìng.

Do you know where I can reserve a train ticket?

At the Information Desk of the hotel.

74

你知道哪儿能————吗？
nǐ zhīdào nǎr néng ma

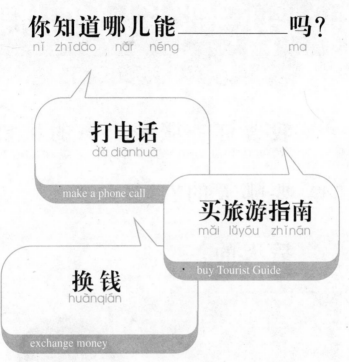

打电话
dǎ diànhuà

make a phone call

买旅游指南
mǎi lǚyóu zhǐnán

buy Tourist Guide

换钱
huànqián

exchange money

Ticket reservation is a very easy thing nowadays. You can make a reservation online or by telephone.

The hot line for air ticket reservations in China is 95105788. In many cities, you can call 114 to inquire about the local ticket reservation hot line number. Online reservation is quite convenient. At http://www.yoee.com you can learn about most international and domestic flights, departure time and discounts.

38

我要订一张去上海的机票。
Wǒ yào dìng yì zhāng qù Shànghǎi de jīpiào.

I want to reserve one air ticket to Shanghai.

● **我要订一张去上海的机票。**
Wǒ yào dìng yì zhāng qù Shànghǎi de jīpiào.

● **要哪天的？**
Yào nǎ tiān de?

● **后天的。**
Hòutiān de.

○ I want to reserve one air ticket to Shanghai.
● For which day?
● For the day after tomorrow.

我要订一张————————。
wǒ yào dìng yì zhāng

去杭州的火车票
qù Hángzhōu de huǒchēpiào

a train ticket to Hangzhou

去广州的软卧
qù Guǎngzhōu de ruǎnwò

a soft sleeper to Guangzhou

明天晚上的电影票
míngtiān wǎnshang de diànyǐngpiào

film ticket for tomorrow evening

Long distance bus: You can easily get a ticket at a low price in a long distance station. The bus might be crowded with local people who are hurry to their own destinations, and the bus may stop several times for passengers to get on and off. But you will see the real life of Chinese people on a long distance bus.

39

有没有今天下午两点到苏州的车票?

Yǒu méiyǒu jīntiān xiàwǔ liǎng diǎn dào Sūzhōu de chēpiào?

Are there any tickets to Suzhou at 2 pm today?

● 有没有今天下午两点到苏州的车票?

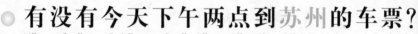

Yǒu méiyǒu jīntiān xiàwǔ liǎng diǎn dào Sūzhōu de chēpiào?

● 对不起，没有了。

Duìbuqǐ, méiyǒu le.

○ Are there any tickets to Suzhou at 2 pm today?
○ Sorry, there aren't.

有没有今天下午两点到____的车票。
yǒu méiyǒu jīntiān xiàwǔ liǎng diǎn dào de chēpiào

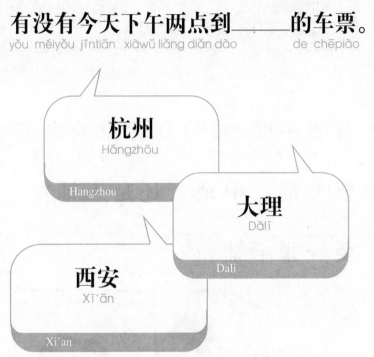

杭州
Hángzhōu

Hangzhou

大理
Dàlǐ

Dali

西安
Xī'ān

Xi'an

There is a booking office in station, and intraday tickets could be bought there if you temporarily decide to go somewhere. You can also buy tickets two days in advance in the booking office of the station.

40

我要一张26号到北京的卧铺票。
Wǒ yào yì zhāng èrshíliù hào dào Běijīng de wòpù piào.

I want a sleeper ticket to Beijing on the 26th.

● 我要一张26号到北京的卧铺票。
Wǒ yào yì zhāng èrshíliù hào dào Běijīng de wòpù piào.

● 要上铺、中铺，还是下铺？
Yào shàngpù, zhōngpù, háishì xiàpù?

● 要一张下铺。
Yào yì zhāng xiàpù.

○ I want a sleeper ticket to Beijing on the 26th.

● Do you want a upper, middle, or lower sleeper?

○ A lower one, please.

我要一张 26 号到北京的————。

wǒ yāo yì zhāng èrshíliù hào dào Běijīng de

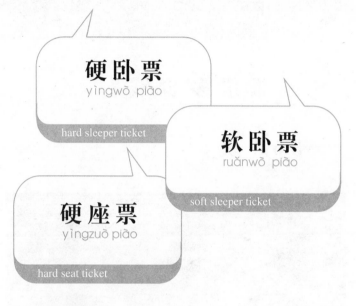

硬卧票
yìngwò piào

hard sleeper ticket

软卧票
ruǎnwò piào

soft sleeper ticket

硬座票
yìngzuò piào

hard seat ticket

DO YOU KNOW?

Traveling by train is one of the cheapest ways to cover long distances and is used widely by the local people. It is important to know what to expect if you decide to travel by train in China.

There are four classes of seats on Chinese trains: hard seat, soft seat, hard sleeper, and soft sleeper. The soft sleeper compartment is a comparative isolated space with better facilities, and soft sleeper ticket is charged a bit less than air ticket. Hard sleepers include upper, middle and lower sleepers. The price of lower sleeper is 10% to 20% higher than the middle and the upper ones.

41

一张票多少钱？

Yì zhāng piào duōshao qián?

How much for one ticket?

一张票多少钱？
Yì zhāng piào duōshao qián?

358 块。
Sānbǎi wǔshíbā kuài.

How much for one ticket?

358 yuan.

———————— **多少钱？**
duōshao qián

一瓶矿泉水
yì píng kuàngquánshuǐ

a bottle of mineral water

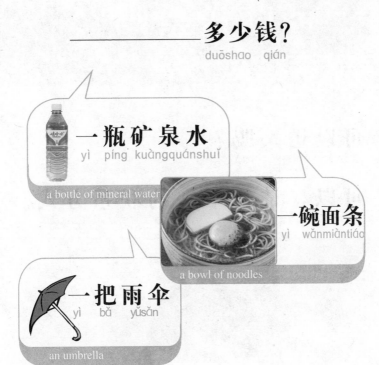

一碗面条
yì wǎnmiàntiáo

a bowl of noodles

一把雨伞
yì bǎ yǔsǎn

an umbrella

The discount for air tickets varies from 20% to 70% according to the different season and departure time. Students with ID cards will get a 50% discount.

42

可以送票吗？
Kěyǐ sòng piào ma?

Can the ticket be delivered?

● 可以送票吗？
Kěyǐ sòng piào ma?

● 可以，请留下您的联系方式。
Kěyǐ, qǐng liúxià nín de liánxì fāngshì.

○ Can the ticket be delivered?
● Yes, please leave your contact details.

可以＿＿＿＿＿＿＿＿吗？
kěyǐ   ma

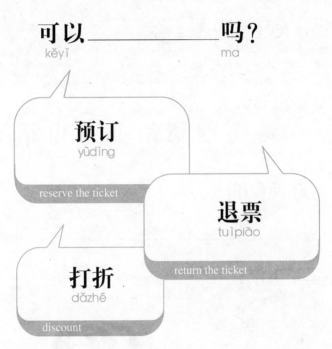

预订
yùdìng

reserve the ticket

退票
tuìpiào

return the ticket

打折
dǎzhé

discount

Ticket delivery for air ticket reservations is available. Delivery in the downtown area is free, but the transportation fare will be charged for delivery to the suburbs. Usually train tickets and bus tickets are not delivered.

85

43

送票前请给我打电话。
Sòng piào qián qǐng gěi wǒ dǎ diànhuà.

Please call me before delivering the ticket.

 送票前请给我打电话。
Sòng piào qián qǐng gěi wǒ dǎ diànhuà.

好的。
Hǎode.

Please call me before delivering the ticket.

OK.

—————前请给我打电话。

qián qǐng gěi wǒ dǎ diànhuà

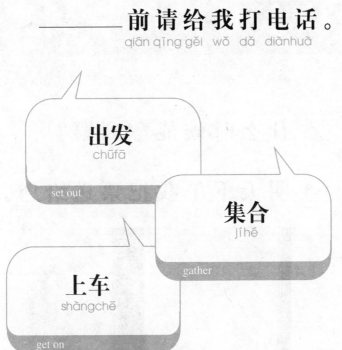

出发
chūfā
set out

集合
jíhé
gather

上车
shàngchē
get on

China Air Transport Association (CATA) has stopped provding paper tickets and instructed sellers to issue e-tickets. Foreign travelers holding e-tickets need only show their passports to board the plane, but they need to ensure that the name on the e-ticket is exactly the same as the name on the passport. A confirmation code will be issued for each e-ticket.

44

什么时候能拿到票？

Shénme shíhou néng nádào piào?

When can I get the ticket?

● 什么时候能拿到票？
Shénme shíhou néng nádào piào?

● 明天下午我把票送给您。
Míngtiān xiàwǔ wǒ bǎ piào sòng gěi nín.

○ When can I get the ticket?
○ I will deliver the ticket to you tomorrow afternoon.

什么时候能————？
shénme shíhou néng

修好
xiūhǎo

repair

到达
dàodá

arrive

结束
jiéshù

finish

Ticket delivery is one of the services of civil aviation. Generally tickets can be delivered within 24 hours. If you have an urgent need, you can ask the civil aviation to provide special service when booking. You pay for the ticket when you receive it.

45

我们几点出发？
Wǒmen jǐ diǎn chūfā?

What time shall we start off?

● **我们几点出发？**
　 Wǒmen jǐ diǎn chūfā?

● **明天早上七点。**
　 Míngtiān zǎoshang qī diǎn.

○ What time shall we start off?
○ At 7 o'clock tomorrow morning.

我们几点 ——————— 。
wǒmen jǐ diǎn

起床
qǐchuáng
get up

吃饭
chīfàn
have dinner

回宾馆
huí bīnguǎn
go back to the hotel

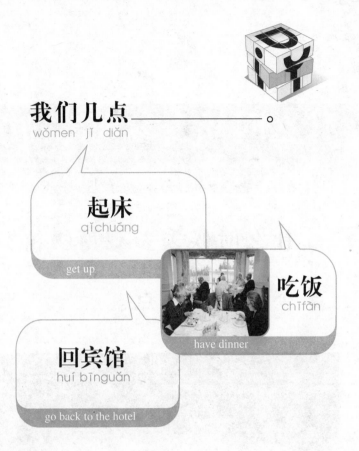

From	To	Air (hour)	Rail (hours)
BEIJING	XI'AN	1.45	11.30
	HARBIN	1.40	10.30
	SHANGHAI	1.55	12.00
	CHONGQING	2.30	24.50
GUANGZHOU	GUILIN	1.00	13.00
	KUNMING	2.15	25.00
SHANGHAI	BEIJING	2.00	12.00
	XI'AN	2.15	16.30
	CHONGQING	2.30	34.20
	KUNMING	2.55	41.00
	GUILIN	2.20	22.45

46

什么时候去参观博物馆?
Shénme shíhou qù cānguān bówùguǎn?

When shall we visit the museum?

什么时候去参观博物馆?
Shénme shíhou qù cānguān bówùguǎn?

今天下午三点。
Jīntiān xiàwǔ sān diǎn.

When shall we visit the museum?

At 3 pm this afternoon.

什么时候去 ————— ?
shénme shíhou qù

逛 古 镇
guàng gǔzhèn

stroll through the old town

买土特产品
mǎi tǔtè chǎnpǐn

buy local products

订火车票
dìng huǒchē piào

reserve a train ticket

For your first visit in China, we recommend Beijing, Xi'an, Shanghai, Guilin, and Tibet, all of which are must-see places. Additionally, some relatively less visited places and routes are also worth seeing. These include: Zhouzhuang Water Village in Suzhou, Hangzhou, Lijiang and Dali Ancient Towns in Yunnan, Pingyao Ancient Town in Shanxi, Yangtze River Cruise, and the Silk Road.

47

一日游有些什么项目？
Yírìyóu yǒu xiē shénme xiàngmù?

What is included on a one-day tour?

○ **一日游有些什么项目？**
Yírìyóu yǒu xiē shénme xiàngmù?

● **有很多项目，我给您介绍一下。**
Yǒu hěn duō xiàngmù, wǒ gěi nín jièshào yíxià.

○ What is included on a one-day tour?

● There are many items. Let me introduce them to you.

有些什么项目？
yǒu xiē shénme xiàngmù

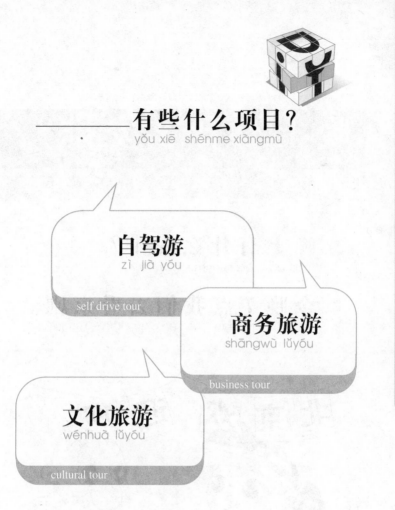

自驾游
zì jià yóu

self drive tour

商务旅游
shāngwù lǚyóu

business tour

文化旅游
wēnhuà lǚyóu

cultural tour

48

晚上有什么安排？
Wǎnshang yǒu shénme ānpái?

What is the plan for the evening?

● 晚上有什么安排？
Wǎnshang yǒu shénme ānpái?

● 今晚 7 点我们去看京剧。
Jīn wǎn qī diǎn wǒmen qù kàn Jīngjù.

What is the plan for the evening?

We are going to see Peking Opera at 7 o'clock this evening.

———有什么安排？
yǒu shénme ānpái

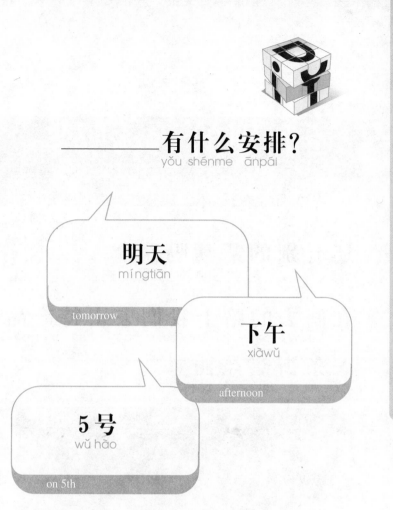

明天
míngtiān

tomorrow

下午
xiàwǔ

afternoon

5 号
wǔ hào

on 5th

Travel agencies seldom arrange activities for tourists in the evening, leaving time for them to stroll the night market or rest in the hotel. If you hope to see a Chinese performance, such as Peking Opera, ask the guide for help.

49

还有别的活动吗？
Hái yǒu bié de huódòng ma?

Are there any other activities?

● 还有别的活动吗？
Hái yǒu bié de huódòng ma?

● 在回去的路上我们去土特产品
Zài huíqù de lùshang wǒmen qù tǔtè chǎnpǐn

一条街买东西。
yìtiáojiē mǎi dōngxi.

○ Are there any other activities?
○ We will stop at the local craft street on the way back.

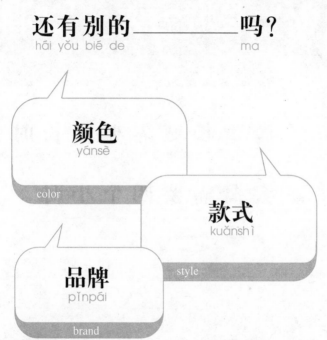

还有别的＿＿＿吗？
hái yǒu bié de　　　　ma

颜色
yánsè

color

款式
kuǎnshì

style

品牌
pǐnpái

brand

The following is a list of the 8 main traditional Chinese festivals:

- **Spring Festival:** on the 1st day of the 1st lunar month, often one month later than the Gregorian calendar.
- **Lantern Festival:** on the 15th day of the 1st lunar month, usually in February or March of the Gregorian calendar.
- **Qingming Festival:** on April 4–6 each year.
- **Dragon Boat Festival:** on the 5th day of the 5th lunar month, usually in June of the Gregorian calendar.
- **Double Seventh Festival:** on the 7th day of the 7th lunar month, usually in August of the Gregorian calendar.
- **Mid-Autumn Festival:** on the 15th day of the 8th lunar month, usually in September or October of the Gregorian calendar.
- **Double Ninth Festival:** on the 9th day of the 9th lunar month, usually in October of the Gregorian calendar.
- **Winter Solstice Festival:** on December 22 or 23 according to the Gregorian calendar.

50

游览长城需要多长时间？

Yóulǎn Chángchéng xūyào duōcháng shíjiān?

How long is the Great Wall excursion?

● 游览长城需要多长时间？
Yóulǎn Chángchéng xūyào duōcháng shíjiān?

● 大概需要四个小时。
Dàgài xūyào sì gè xiǎoshí.

◯ How long is the Great Wall excursion?
◯ It takes about 4 hours.

需要多长时间？
xūyào duōcháng shíjiān

参观故宫
cānguān Gùgōng

visit the Palace Museum

到下一个景点
dào xià yí gè jǐngdiǎn

get to the next scenic spot

去黄山
qù Huángshān

go to Huangshan Mountain

DO YOU KNOW

The Great Wall is about 6300 kilometers long, running from Shanhaiguan in the east to Jiayuguan in the west. The Great Wall in Beijing is about 600 kilometers long. The famous passes are Badaling, Jinshanling, Simatai, Mutianyu and Juyongguan. The Great Wall in Beijing was built in 1540 during the Ming Dynasty in China, and it has lasted more than 460 years.

51

改一下明天的日程吧。
Gǎi yíxià míngtiān de rìchéng ba.

Shall we change the schedule for tomorrow?

🔵 **改一下明天的日程吧。**
Gǎi yíxià míngtiān de rìchéng ba.

🔵 **你想怎么改呢？**
Nǐ xiǎng zěnme gǎi ne?

🔵 Shall we change the schedule for tomorrow?
🔵 How would you like to change it?

改一下 ＿＿＿＿＿ 吧。
gǎi yíxià ba

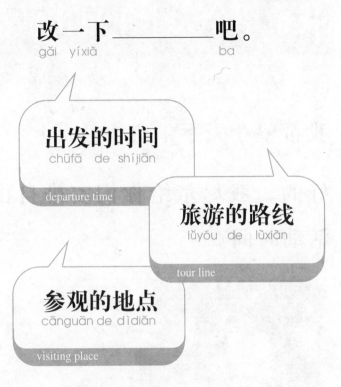

出发的时间
chūfā de shíjiān

departure time

旅游的路线
lǚyóu de lùxiàn

tour line

参观的地点
cānguān de dìdiǎn

visiting place

Chinese folklore is rich and varied, and more than 40 Chinese festivals are known throughout the world. Not a month passes without a festival being observed among one ethnic group or another. If you happen to be in a place on the day of a festival, don't miss it. Ask the guide to change your travel schedule if necessary.

52

我希望今天下午自由活动。
Wǒ xīwàng jīntiān xiàwǔ zìyóu huódòng.

I hope we have free time this afternoon.

- 我希望今天下午自由活动。
  Wǒ xīwàng jīntiān xiàwǔ zìyóu huódòng.

- 好的，我尽量给你们安排自由
  Hǎode, wǒ jǐnliàng gěi nǐmen ānpái zìyóu

  活动时间。
  huódòng shíjiān.

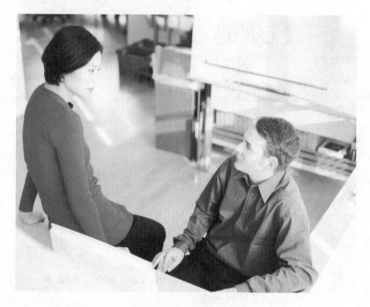

- I hope we have free time this afternoon.
- OK, I will try my best to arrange free time for you.

104

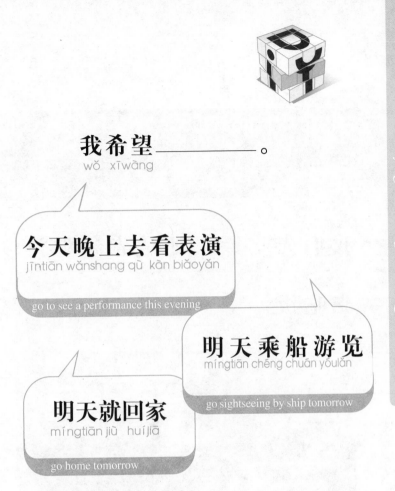

我希望————————。
wǒ xīwàng

今天晚上去看表演
jīntiān wǎnshang qù kàn biǎoyǎn

go to see a performance this evening

明天乘船游览
míngtiān chéng chuán yóulǎn

go sightseeing by ship tomorrow

明天就回家
míngtiān jiù huíjiā

go home tomorrow

Peking Opera, Chinese acrobatics, music, dance, and traditional Chinese painting and calligraph—these never fail to bring immense joy to visitors from all over the world. If they are not included in your travel plans, make sure that you have enough time to enjoy them in the free time scheduled for your travel group.

我们先吃饭，还是先参观?

Wǒmen xiān chīfàn, háishi xiān cānguān?

Shall we go to eat first or go to visit first?

我们先吃饭，还是先参观?
Wǒmen xiān chī fàn, háishi xiān cānguān?

先吃饭。
Xiān chīfàn.

Shall we go to eat first or go to visit first?

We will go to eat first.

我们先———，还是先参观？
wǒmen xiān　　　　　　　háishi xiān cānguān

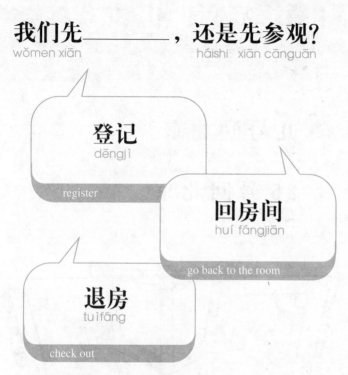

登记
dēngjì

register

回房间
huí fángjiān

go back to the room

退房
tuìfáng

check out

The Chinese tourism industry is not only rich in resources; it has also come a long way in transportation, service, accommodation, catering and shopping facilities, and recreation. Tourist facilities are being constantly improved, and so is the service. With a winsome smile the hospitable Chinese are trusted companions for those traveling in China.

54

几号回北京？
Jǐ hāo huí Běijīng?

On which date shall we go back to Beijing?

○ **几号回北京？**
Jǐ hāo huí Běijīng?

○ **25号回北京。**
Èrshí wǔ hāo huí Běijīng.

○ On which date shall we go back to Beijing?

○ We will go back to Beijing on the 25th.

几号————?
jǐ hǎo

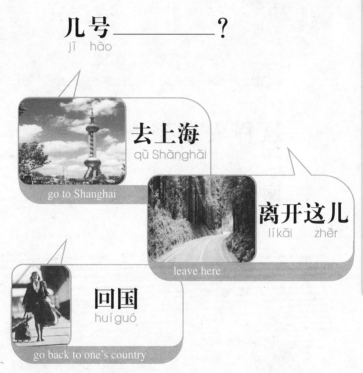

去上海
qù Shànghǎi
go to Shanghai

离开这儿
lí kāi zhèr
leave here

回国
huí guó
go back to one's country

Recommended China Tourist City Guide List
(listed alphabetically)

Beijing Chengdu Chongqing Dali Dalian Dunhuang
Guangzhou Guilin Hangzhou Jinan Kunming Lhasa
Lijiang Luoyang Nanjing Pingyao Qingdao Shanghai
Shenzhen Suzhou Tianjin Wuhan Wuxi Xi'an
Xining Xishuangbanna Yangshuo Yangzhou
Zhouzhuang

55

这样安排很合理。
Zhèyàng ānpái hěn hélǐ.

The schedule is very reasonable.

这样安排**很合理**。
Zhèyàng ānpái hěn hélǐ.

 谢谢。
Xièxie.

The schedule is very reasonable.

Thank you.

110

这样安排————。
zhèyàng ānpái

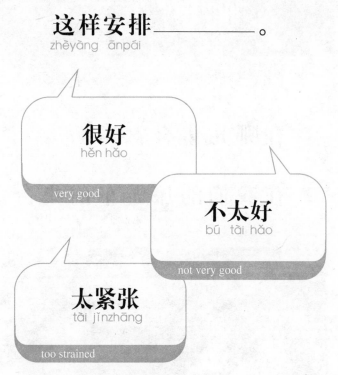

很好
hěn hǎo

very good

不太好
bú tài hǎo

not very good

太紧张
tài jǐnzhāng

too strained

Travel agencies in China have many multi-destination tour packages as well as many city packages to single destinations like Beijing, Xi'an, Guilin, Shanghai, Hong Kong, Yangtze River, Tibet etc. No matter who you are, whether an independent traveler, couple, family or group, just select the tour that suits you.

111

56

在哪儿集合？
Zài   nǎr   jíhé?

Where shall we meet?

在哪儿集合？
Zài   nǎr   jíhé?

在我们的旅游车前集合。
Zài   wǒmen de   lǚyóu   chē qián   jíhé.

Where shall we meet?

We will meet in front of our bus.

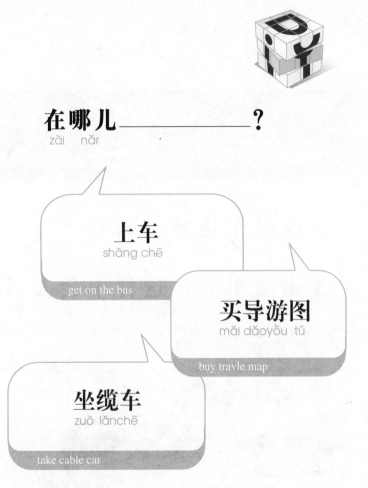

在哪儿————?
zài nǎr

上车
shàng chē
get on the bus

买导游图
mǎi dǎoyóu tú
buy travle map

坐缆车
zuò lǎnchē
take cable car

DO YOU KNOW?

Join a group and visit the most popular places before you explore this huge special world on your own. With a mind for adventure and good will, expect minor changes or rough patches due to cultural or material differences, relax yourself and enjoy your trip. The Chinese people are friendly to foreign visitors, and your guides would be trained, experienced and most reliable. Follow your guide's directions and your trip will be smooth and enjoyable.

57

坐缆车还是走路？
Zuò lǎnchē háishi zǒulù?

Shall we take the cable car or walk?

○ **坐缆车还是走路？**
Zuò lǎnchē háishi zǒulù?

● **坐缆车吧，这样不会太累。**
Zuò lǎnchē ba, zhèyàng bú huì tài lèi.

 Shall we take the cable car or walk?

● Let's take the cable car so that we will not be too tired.

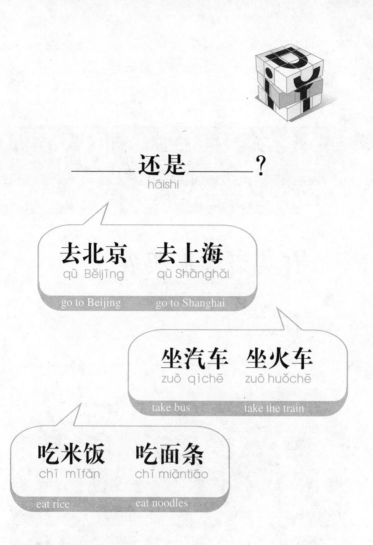

_____还是_____?
háishi

去北京　去上海
qù Běijīng　qù Shànghǎi
go to Beijing　go to Shanghai

坐汽车　坐火车
zuò qìchē　zuò huǒchē
take bus　take the train

吃米饭　吃面条
chī mǐfàn　chī miàntiáo
eat rice　eat noodles

China is a very safe place for foreigners to visit. Even minor crimes are punished severely, especially if related to foreigners. Venders at some sightseeing locations may be persistent but are usually polite. Just ignore them if you don't want to buy something. If you travel with a guide, just follow him/her. If you explore alone, be alert and use common sense.

58

有英语导游吗？
Yǒu Yīngyǔ dǎoyóu ma?

Is there an English guide?

有英语导游吗？
Yǒu Yīngyǔ dǎoyóu ma?

有。
Yǒu.

Is there an English guide?
Yes.

有————导游吗?
yǒu　　　　　dǎo yóu ma

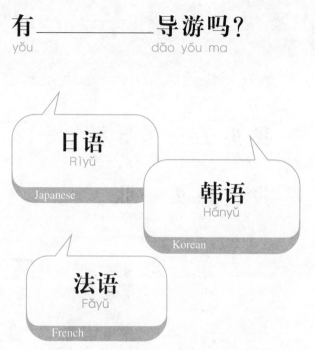

日语
Rìyǔ

Japanese

韩语
Hányǔ

Korean

法语
Fǎyǔ

French

Not all the tourist sites provide foreign language guides. If you want to know something in detail, such as the history and culture of the place, you'd better ask a foreign language guide to make professional introduction. The foreign guide service is charged by working hours, usually at approximately 20−30 yuan per hour.

59

我买了一张导游图。

Wǒ mǎi le yì zhāng dǎoyóu tú.

I bought a tourist map.

- 我买了一张导游图。
  Wǒ mǎi le yì zhāng dǎoyóu tú.

- 我也想买一张。
  Wǒ yě xiǎng mǎi yì zhāng.

- I bought a tourist map.
- I want to buy one, too.

我买了———————。
wǒ mǎi le

一个纪念品
yí gè jìniànpǐn

a souvenir

一套明信片
yí tào míngxìnpiàn

a set of post cards

一本旅游指南
yì běn lǚyóu zhǐnán

a tourist guide

China has tens of thousands of trained and licensed tour guides. Some of them are professors, librarians, and teachers working in their free time. There are tour guide exams once each year, and only those who pass are qualified to work. China's travel companies are categorized into three classes. Class 1 can work directly with foreign tour operators. Tour guides working for this class are usually more experienced. English is the primary foreign language spoken by most tour guides.

这里的风景真美啊！

Zhèlǐ de fēngjǐng zhēn měi a!

How beautiful the scenery here is!

这里的风景真美啊！
Zhèlǐ de fēngjǐ zhēn měi a!

真的很美。
Zhēn de hěn měi.

How beautiful the scenery here is!

It really is.

这里的 _____ 啊！
zhělǐ de a

天真蓝
tiān zhēn lán
the sky is very blue

水真清
shuǐ zhēn qīng
the water is very clear

东西真好吃
dōngxi zhēn hǎochī
the food is very delicious

Traditional Chinese life is presented in many places. When traveling in China, hutongs in Beijing or the small water villages of Qingpu near Shanghai will show you vivid traditional Chinese lifestyle. If you have time and really want to see relatively untouched traditional culture, you can go to China's remote western areas. Dali and Lijiang in Yunnan province, along with Tibet, are great places where age-old traditions are well preserved.

61

我喜欢这里。
Wǒ xǐhuan zhèlǐ.

I like here very much.

- 我喜欢这里。
  Wǒ xǐhuan zhèlǐ.

- 我也是。
  Wǒ yě shì.

I like here very much.

Me, too.

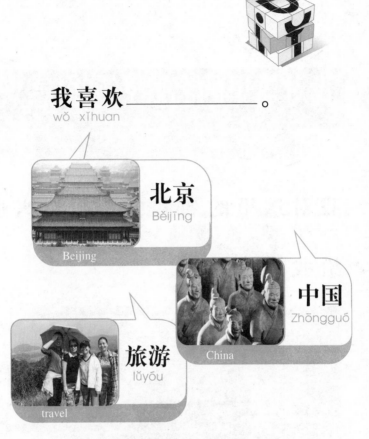

我喜欢 ——————————。
wǒ xǐhuan

北京
Běijīng
Beijing

中国
Zhōngguó
China

旅游
lǚyóu
travel

DO YOU KNOW?

Tibet's high altitude and the atmosphere allow the sun's solar radiation to strike the earth with unusual intensity. To protect your eyes and skin, sunscreen, sunglasses and lip cream are advised. In addition to the normal medications for traveling, such as Aspirin and Ibuprofen, you should bring some "high altitude medication". It's better to ask your doctor for suggestions.

62

我对这里的名胜古迹很感兴趣。

Wǒ duì zhèlǐ de míngshèng gǔjì hěn gǎn xìngqù.

I am very interested in the scenic spots and historical sites here.

● 我对这里的名胜古迹很感兴趣。
Wǒ duì zhèlǐ de míngshèng gǔjì hěn gǎn xìngqù.

● 给我讲讲吧。
Gěi wǒ jiǎngjiang ba.

○ I am very interested in the scenic spots and historical sites here.

○ Tell me something about them.

我对这里的————很感兴趣。
wǒ duì zhèlǐ de   hěn gǎn xìngqù

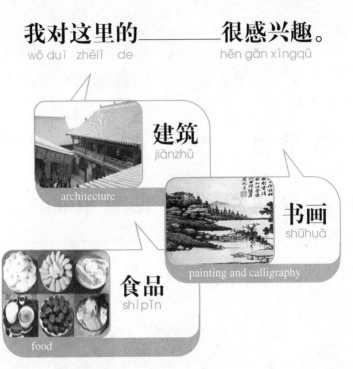

建筑
jiànzhù

architecture

书画
shūhuà

painting and calligraphy

食品
shípǐn

food

Sightseeing ◉ 观光

DO YOU KNOW?

If Beijing is the political heart of China, then Xi'an is its historical center. An ancient philosopher once mused that all those seeking the truth should go to China. A contemporary philosopher added that no visit to China is complete without a journey to Xi'an. Xi'an holds as a famed historical and cultural city and as one of China's six major ancient capitals. The most famous scenic spots and historical sites of Xi'an include: Museum of Terracotta Warriors, Mausoleum of Emperor Qinshihuang, Forest of Stone Stales, and the Big & Small Goose Pagodas.

我 觉 得 一 般 。
Wǒ juéde yìbān.
I think it's so-so.

我 觉 得 一 般 。
Wǒ juéde yìbān.

我 也 觉 得 没 有 我 想 象 的 好 。
Wǒ yě juéde méiyǒu wǒ xiǎngxiàng de hǎo.

I think it's so-so.
I don't think it's as good as what I expected, either.

63

126

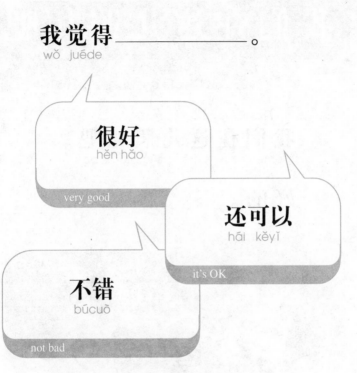

我觉得———————。
wǒ juéde

很好
hěn hǎo
very good

还可以
hái kěyǐ
it's OK

不错
búcuò
not bad

DO YOU KNOW?

The Silk Road linked China and the western world in 138 B.C. when Zhangqian, the first explorer of ancient China, started his exploration from the Central Kingdom of Xihan Dynasty to the outside world with China wares and silk. Though given a pretty name by Marco Polo, the Silk Road included deadly terrain and a lengthy pass through the desert. The Silk Road was not only a trading route, but also a cultural link between China and the western countries. It is absolutely not a so-so tour.

64

我们在这儿照相吧。

Wǒmen　zài　zhěr　zhǎoxiàng　ba.

Let's take a picture here.

● 我们在这儿照相吧。
　Wǒmen　zài　zhěr　zhǎoxiàng ba.

● 好的。
　Hǎode.

 Let's take a picture here.

● OK.

我们在这儿————吧。
wǒmen zài zhèr   ba

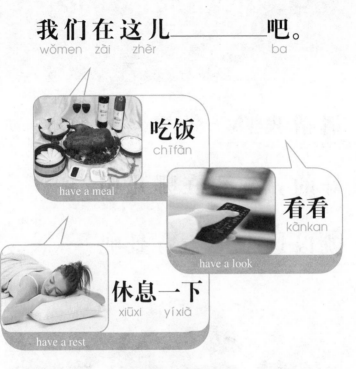

吃饭
chīfàn

have a meal

看看
kànkan

have a look

休息一下
xiūxi   yí xià

have a rest

Five most famous mountains in China
Hengshan, South Yue in Hunan Province
Hengshan, North Yue in Shanxi Province
Huashan, West Yue in Shaanxi Province
Taishan, East Yue in Shandong Province
Songshan, Central Yue in Henan Province

65

请帮我照一张相。

Qǐng bāng wǒ zhào yì zhāng xiāng.

Please take a picture for me.

● **请帮我照一张相。**
Qǐng bāng wǒ zhào yì zhāng xiàng.

● **好的，你想在哪儿照？**
Hǎode, nǐ xiǎng zài nǎr zhào?

● **就以这个塔为背景吧。**
Jiù yǐ zhège tǎ wéi bèijǐng ba.

○ Please take a picture for me.
○ OK, where do you want to take the picture?
○ Take this tower as background.

请 帮 我 ——————。
qǐng bāng wǒ

买一瓶水
mǎi yì píng shuǐ

buy a bottle of water

看一下包
kān yíxià bāo

keep an eye on the bag

打一个电话
dǎ yí gè diànhuà

make a phone call

Photo taking is not allowed in some temples. You'd better ask before taking a photo. The most recommended temples for the tourists are: Confucius–Qufu, Shandong; Dazu Buddhist–Chongqing; Xiangshan and Biyun–Beijing; Yungang Grottoes–Datong, Shanxi.

66

一、二、三，"茄子"。

Yī, èr, sān, "qiézi".

One, two, three, "qiezi".

○ 一、二、三，"茄子"。
　　Yī,　　èr,　　sān,　　"qiézi".

○ "茄子"。
　　"Qiézi".

○ One, two, three, "qiezi".

○ "Qiezi".

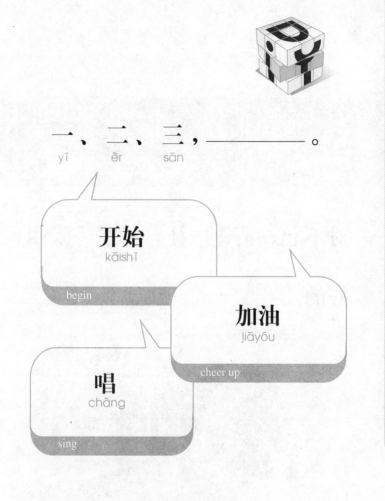

一、二、三，————。
yī　ěr　sān

开始
kāishǐ
begin

加油
jiāyóu
cheer up

唱
chàng
sing

DO YOU KNOW?

Like "cheese" in English, "qiézi (eggplant)" is always used when taking pictures since when we say "qiézi", we have smiling faces.

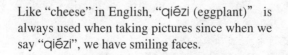

对不起，请让一让，我照一张相。
Duìbuqǐ, qǐng ràng yi ràng, wǒ zhào yì zhāng xiàng.

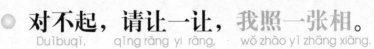
Sorry, please move. I am going to take a picture.

对不起，请让一让，我照一张相。
Duìbuqǐ, qǐng ràng yi ràng, wǒ zhào yì zhāng xiàng.

好的。
Hǎode.

Sorry, please move. I am going to take a picture.

OK.

对不起，请让一让，————。
duìbuqǐ　　qǐng ràng yi ràng

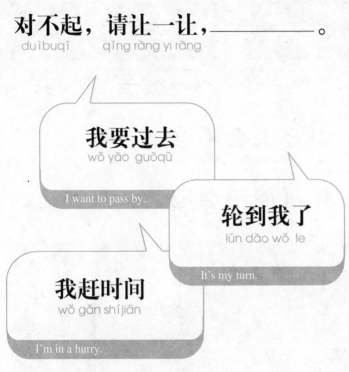

我要过去
wǒ yào guòqù

I want to pass by.

轮到我了
lún dào wǒ le

It's my turn.

我赶时间
wǒ gǎn shíjiān

I'm in a hurry.

There are usually many tourists at scenic points. If the view you want to take is blocked by tourists, you can politely ask him/her to move. "Qǐng ràng yi ràng" could also be used in some crowded situations when you want to pass by quickly.

今天会不会下雨?

Jīntiān huì bú huì xià yǔ?

Is it going to rain today?

今天会不会下雨?

Jīntiān huì bú huì xià yǔ?

可能不会吧。

Kěnéng bú huì ba.

Is it going to rain today?

It is not likely to rain.

今天会不会————?
jīntiān huì bú huì

下雪
xià xuě

snow

刮风
guā fēng

windy

有沙尘
yǒu shāchén

sandy

DO YOU KNOW

China's weather varies from tropical in the far south to sub-arctic in the far north. China is a big landmass, running from the Pacific to the Himalayas. It's about 5 500 kilometers from the tropical south to the cooler north, and there can be as much as 40℃ difference between them. In winter the wind blows from Siberia, bringing very cold, dry weather in the north, but weakening as it travels south; while in summer the wind brings warm wet weather from the ocean, and summers can be very hot and humid in many areas. Spring and autumn usually bring the best weather.

明天是晴天吗？

Míngtiān shì qíngtiān ma?

Will it be a fine day tomorrow?

● 明天是晴天吗？

Míngtiān shì qíngtiān ma?

● 明天是个大晴天。

Míngtiān shì gè dà qíngtiān.

Will it be a fine day tomorrow?

It will be a fine day tomorrow.

明天 ——— 吗？
míngtiān　　　　　ma

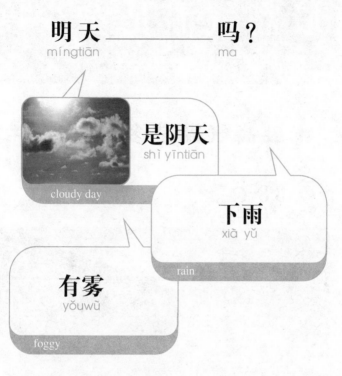

是阴天
shì yīntiān

cloudy day

下雨
xià yǔ

rain

有雾
yǒuwù

foggy

DO YOU KNOW

May, September and October are the peak tourist months at most of China's popular destinations as the weather is most comfortable, but prices are higher and everywhere is more crowded. Prices drop a bit from late March through April and from June through August. The slow season arrives in late November and continues through the winter, when there are fewer crowds and the prices are lower.

70

最高气温是多少度？
Zuì gāo qìwēn shì duōshao dù?

What is the highest temperature?

最高气温是多少度？
Zuì gāo qìwēn shì duōshao dù?

38℃。
Sānshíbā shèshìdù.

What is the highest temperature?

38℃.

气温是多少度？
qìwēn shì duōshǎo dù

最低
zuì dī

the lowest

平均
píngjūn

average

In China, the temperature is always showed by Celsius(℃). The conversion formula between Fahrenheit and Celsius is °F=9/5℃ +32. The so-called four hot centers of China are Chongqing, Nanjing, Wuhan and Changsha. The highest temperature there is at about 42℃ in summer.

71

外面很热吧？
Wàimian hěn rè ba?

Is it very hot outside?

○ **外面很热吧？**
Wàimian hěn rè ba?

○ **不太热。**
Bú tài rè.

○ Is it very hot outside?

○ Not very hot.

外面 ——————— 吧？
wàimian   ba

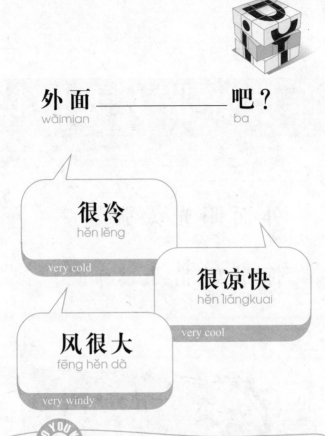

很冷
hěn lěng

very cold

很凉快
hěn liángkuai

very cool

风很大
fēng hěn dà

very windy

China has a continental and seasonal climate. Most parts are in the temperate zone, but southern areas are in the tropical or subtropical zone, while northern areas are in the frigid zone. Climates in different areas are complicated. For instance, northern Heilongjiang province has a winter climate year-round, while Hainan Island has a summer climate year-round. The following is a reference table for tourists to consult when preparing clothing for their trips.

Spring: 10℃-22℃, Western suits, jackets, sport coats, woolen jackets, long sleeve shirts and travel shoes.

Summer: 22℃ and above, T-shirts, short sleeve shirts, skirts, sandals, caps, rain gear.

Autumn: 10℃-22℃, Western suits, jackets, sport coats, light woolen sweaters, rain gear and travel shoes.

Winter: 10℃ or lower, overcoat, cotton clothes, lined coats. In very cold areas a cap, gloves and cotton-padded shoes are required.

Weather ● 天气

72

你最好带上太阳镜。
Nǐ zuìhǎo dài shang tàiyángjìng.

You'd better wear your sunglasses.

- 外面阳光太强了。
  Wàimian yángguāng tài qiáng le.

- 你最好带上太阳镜。
  Nǐ zuìhǎo dàishang tàiyángjìng.

- The sunlight is too strong outside.
- You'd better wear your sunglasses.

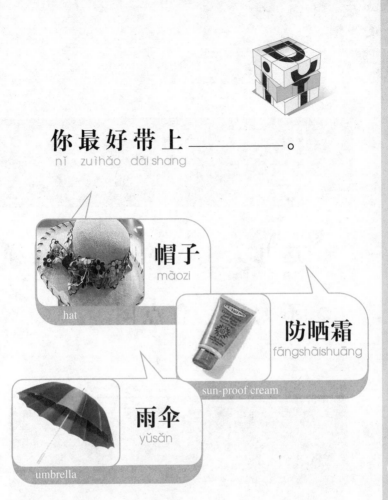

你 最 好 带 上 ——————。
nǐ zuìhǎo dài shang

帽子
mǎozi

hat

防晒霜
fángshàishuāng

sun-proof cream

雨伞
yǔsǎn

umbrella

Cycling through China will provide meaningful and enjoyable travel experiences at a reasonable cost. There is no better way to see China than from the seat of your bicycle, riding from village to town to city through the fascinating countryside. Many cycling tour companies offer affordable tours, great service and fantastic routes. The trips are fun, exciting, challenging and rewarding for experienced touring cyclists.

73

这几天上海的天气怎么样？

Zhè jǐ tiān Shànghǎi de tiānqì zěnmeyàng?

How's the weather in Shanghai these days?

● 这几天上海的天气怎么样？

Zhè jǐ tiān Shànghǎi de tiānqì zěnmeyàng?

● 不太好，有点闷。

Bú tài hǎo, yǒu diǎn mēn.

● How's the weather in Shanghai these days?

● It's not so good. It's a little bit stuffy.

这几天＿＿＿的天气怎么样？
zhè jǐ tiān ＿＿＿ de tiānqì zěnmeyàng

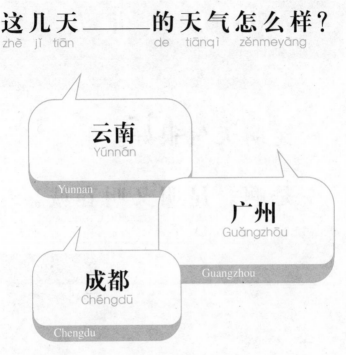

云南
Yúnnán
Yunnan

广州
Guǎngzhōu
Guangzhou

成都
Chéngdū
Chengdu

China is a large country which covers frigid-temperate, temperate, sub-torrid and torrid zones from the south to the north. The climate of southwest and northwest China is typical mesa and mountain climate. Because of the huge topography change, there is a saying in the southwest that "a mountain shows four seasons and the weather is different within 5 kilometers", which means the climate changes a lot in this area. You'd better check the weather conditions in advance when you travel.

147

74

昆明天气很好。
Kūnmíng tiānqì hěn hǎo.

The weather is nice in Kunming.

○ 昆明天气很好。
Kūnmíng tiānqì hěn hǎo.

● 是啊，昆明又叫春城。
Shì a, Kūnmíng yòu jiào chūnchéng.

 The weather is nice in Kunming.

○ Yes, Kunming is also known as "spring city".

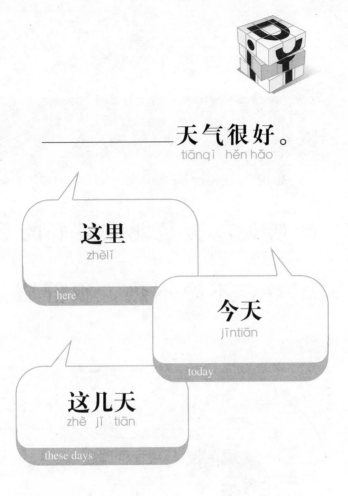

————天气很好。
tiānqì hěn hǎo

这里
zhèlǐ
here

今天
jīntiān
today

这儿天
zhè jǐ tiān
these days

Kunming is the capital city of Yunnan province. Because the weather there is nice year-round, it is called the "spring city". Some cities in China have their own special names according to their weather conditions. For example, Harbin is called the "ice city" because of its unique ice sculptures in winter, and Chongqing is called the "fog city" because of its heavy fog.

75

听说秋天是北京最好的季节。

Tīngshuō qiūtiān shì Běijīng zuì hǎo de jìjié.

It is said that autumn is the best season in Beijing.

● 听说秋天是北京最好的季节。
　　Tīngshuō qiūtiān shì Běijīng zuì hǎo de jìjié.

● 对，不冷不热，很舒服。
　　Duì, bù lěng bú rè, hěn shūfu.

● It is said that autumn is the best season in Beijing.
● Yes, it is neither cold nor hot. It's very nice.

听说————是北京最好的季节。
tīngshuō　　　　　shì Běijīng zuì hǎo de　jìjié

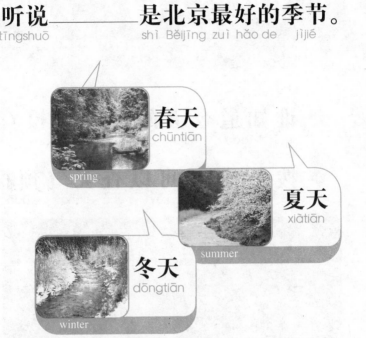

春天
chūntiān

spring

夏天
xiàtiān

summer

冬天
dōngtiān

winter

Selecting the best season is important to tourists. For example, when you come to Beijing in autumn, you will be impressed by Beijing as a beautiful city with clear air and fine weather. But if you visit Beijing in spring, you will see the whole city is covered in sand and dust.

Weather ● 天气

76

谁知道今天的天气预报？
Shuí zhīdào jīntiān de tiānqì yùbào?

Who knows today's weather forecast?

● 谁知道今天的天气预报？
Shuí zhīdào jīntiān de tiānqì yùbào?

● 拨12121可以查天气预报。
Bō yāo'èryāo'èryāo kěyǐ chá tiānqì yùbào.

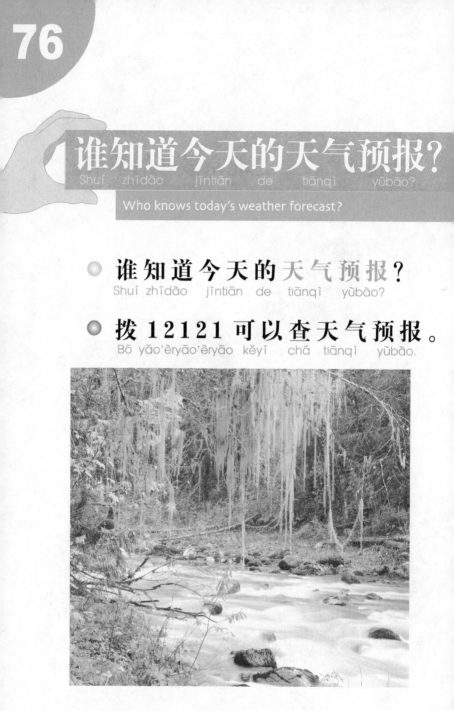

○ Who knows today's weather forecast?
○ Dial 12121 to check the weather forecast.

谁知道今天的 _____？
shuí zhīdào jīntiān de

日程安排
rìchéng ānpái

daily agenda

交通情况
jiāotōng qíngkuàng

traffic situation

出发时间
chūfā shíjiān

departure time

Weather forecast information can be consulted in the following ways: daily newspapers, TV programs, broadcasts, mobile messages or telephone. If you want to know the long-term weather forecast, get the information from http://www.t7online.com.

77

我想买些特产。

Wǒ xiǎng mǎi xiē tèchǎn.

I want to buy some local specialty products.

● **我想买些特产。**
Wǒ xiǎng mǎi xiē tèchǎn.

● **我们去特产商店看看吧。**
Wǒmen qù tèchǎn shāngdiàn kànkan ba.

I want to buy some local specialty products.

Let's go to local products shop.

我想买些 ———。
wǒ xiǎng mǎi xiē

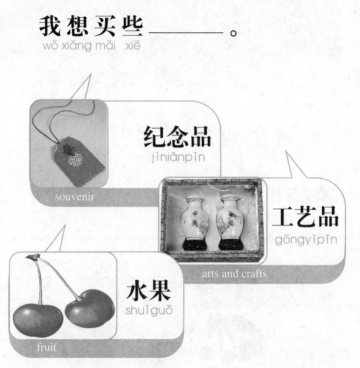

纪念品
jìniànpǐn

souvenir

工艺品
gōngyìpǐn

arts and crafts

水果
shuǐguǒ

fruit

You won't have any problems finding an ATM in China's bigger cities, but you probably won't be able to find one in remote areas or smaller towns. However, this situation is changing, and ATMs are gradually spreading across the country.

78

这个包怎么卖？
Zhège bāo zěnme mǎi?

How much is the bag?

● 这个包怎么卖？
　Zhège bāo zěnme mǎi?

● 50 块。
　Wǔshí kuài.

工艺品专卖

 How much is the bag?

● 50 yuan.

———怎么卖？
zěnme mǎi

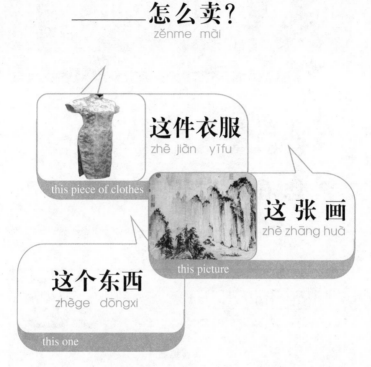

这件衣服
zhè jiàn yīfu

this piece of clothes

这张画
zhè zhāng huà

this picture

这个东西
zhège dōngxi

this one

"Zěnme mǎi" can be used as "duōshao qián" for asking price. "Dōngxi" is a general term in Chinese. When shopping, we can say we are going to "mǎi dōngxi". If you don't know how to translate the things you want to buy, you can point at it and call it "zhège dōngxi".

79

我 想 买 几 张 明 信 片。
Wǒ xiǎng mǎi jǐ zhāng míngxìnpiàn.

I want to buy some post cards.

 我 想 买 几 张 明 信 片。
Wǒ xiǎng mǎi jǐ zhāng míngxìnpiàn.

 您 看 看 这 种 吧。
Nín kānkan zhè zhǒng ba.

中国邮政明信片
Postcard
The people's Republic of China

1 0 0 0 6 6

60分

Happy New Year,
Wish you happy

北京市西城区德外大街4号

高等教育出版社

国际汉语出版中心　收

邮政编码　100011

 I want to buy some post cards.
Take a look at this one.

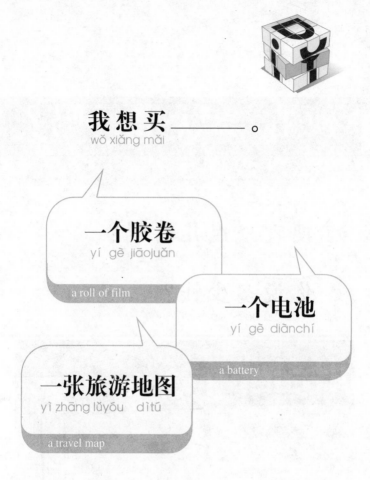

我 想 买 ————。
wǒ xiǎng mǎi

一个胶卷
yí gè jiāojuǎn

a roll of film

一个电池
yí gè diànchí

a battery

一张旅游地图
yì zhāng lǚyóu dìtú

a travel map

Shopping Guide in China
- Do not shop for everything you want in a single city.
- Do not feel obligated to shop.
- Shop in the market or local department store.
- Be a smart consumer.

80

便宜一点儿行吗？
Piányi yìdiǎnr xíng ma?

Could you go a little cheaper?

● 便宜一点儿行吗？
Piányi yìdiǎnr xíng ma?

● 你说多少钱？
Nǐ shuō duōshao qián?

○ Could you go a little cheaper?
○ What is your price?

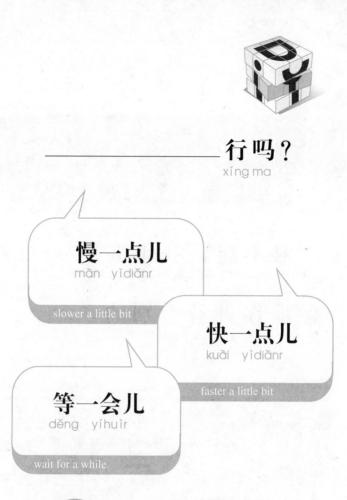

———————— 行吗？
xíng ma

慢一点儿
màn yìdiǎnr

slower a little bit

快一点儿
kuài yìdiǎnr

faster a little bit

等一会儿
děng yíhuìr

wait for a while

DO YOU KNOW?

In China, bargaining is normally acceptable except in large department stores, expensive boutiques and restaurants.

Here is some advice on how to bargain：

Have a general idea of the common price (you can visit different shops to check the average price).

A 50% discount is widely acceptable in China, so offer half the price the vendor asks. When you are presented with a good price after bargaining, you should buy the item, otherwise you will be regarded to be impolite and dishonest.

81

对 不 起， 我 不 要 了。

Duìbuqǐ, wǒ bú yào le.

Sorry, I don't want to buy it.

● 对 不 起， 我 不 要 了。
　 Duìbuqǐ, wǒ bú yào le.

● 那 你 再 看 看 别 的。
　 Nà nǐ zài kànkan bié de.

○ Sorry, I don't want to buy it.
● Then have a look at other things.

对不起，我不____了。
duìbuqǐ, wǒ bú le

试
shì

try

去
qù

go

看
kàn

look

Cautions for Foreigners Buying Chinese Antiques
- When buying expensive articles, choose the shops run by the state.
- Make sure that the antiques you bought carry a wax seal indicating that they are authentic and are able to be exported from China.
- Know that antiques dating before 1795 cannot be legally exported.
- Keep the purchase receipts. You will be asked to present them by customs when leaving China.

82

可以刷卡吗？

Kěyǐ shuākǎ ma?

Can I use a credit card?

● 可以刷卡吗？
Kěyǐ shuākǎ ma?

● 可以，请到付款台刷卡。
Kěyǐ, qǐng dào fùkuǎntái shuākǎ.

○ Can I use a credit card?
○ Yes, please go to the payment desk to pay by credit card.

可以_____吗？
kěyǐ　　　　ma

用美元
yòng Měiyuán

use American dollar

用外币
yòng wàibì

use foreign currency

用现金
yòng xiànjīn

use cash

Taking a credit card with you when you are traveling is very convenient now. International credit cards, such as Visa, MasterCard, Diners Club and GNS are often accepted in some big marketplaces, supermarkets and hotels in China. You can withdraw money from ATMs in some big cities with the above-mentioned cards, but you are often charged about 1% charge because of withdrawing out of your country.

83

在哪儿可以换钱?

Zài nǎr kěyǐ huàn qián?

Where can I exchange money?

- 在哪儿可以换钱?
  Zài nǎr kěyǐ huàn qián?

- 在银行或者宾馆都可以。
  Zài yínháng huòzhě bīnguǎn dōu kěyǐ.

- Where can I exchange money?
- You can exchange money in a bank or hotel.

在哪儿可以————————?
zài nǎr kěyǐ

买车票
mǎi chēpiào

buy a train ticket

上网
shàngwǎng

surf the internet

打电话
dǎ diànhuà

make a phone call

The Bank of China provides exchange service for USD, GBP, AUD, CAD, EUR, HKD, JPY, and SGD. The exchange rate may be different everyday. You can check it from the exchange rate board in the bank, online at http://www.hsbc.com.cn or by calling 8008302880.

84

请给我发票。

Qǐng gěi wǒ fāpiào.

Please give me a receipt.

请给我发票。
Qǐng gěi wǒ fāpiào.

没问题。
Méi wèntí.

Please give me a receipt.
No problem.

请给我 ——————— 。
qǐng gěi wǒ

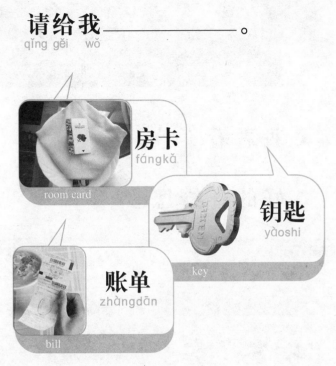

房卡
fángkǎ

room card

钥匙
yàoshi

key

账单
zhàngdān

bill

DO YOU KNOW?

Don't forget to ask for the receipt when you go shopping in case you need to return or exchange the item you bought due to quality problems or if you are not satisfied. You can call 12315 to complain about fake articles or poor quality.

85

我看看菜单。
Wǒ kànkan cǎidān.

Let me have a look at the menu.

● **我看看菜单。**
Wǒ kànkan cǎidān.

● **好的，给您。**
Hǎode, gěi nín.

主食　　　　　　　　　　　　　　　　　　　　**主食**

饼类

葱花饼：	16元／份
葱油饼加鸡蛋：	18元／份
麻香葱油饼：	18元／份
韭菜盒子：	21元／份

← 锅贴：21元／份

家常饼：16元／份 →

米饭

扬州炒饭：	33元／份
小葱蛋炒饭：	26元／份
白米饭：	5元／碗
韩国豆饭：	8元／碗

水饺

韭菜鸡蛋：	43元／斤
猪肉大葱：	43元／斤
猪肉茴香：	43元／斤
西葫芦鸡蛋：	43元／斤

甜食

炸红薯饼： 25元／份
炸南瓜饼： 25元／份
香芋芝麻卷： 21元／份
豆沙麻团： 21元／份

烤红薯：26元／份
煮玉米：26元／份
果味面包夹：21元／份

面条

老北京炸酱面：	36元／盆
西红柿打卤面：	36元／盆
热汤面：	33元／盆

○ Let me have a look at the menu.
● OK, here you are.

我看看_____。
wǒ kànkan

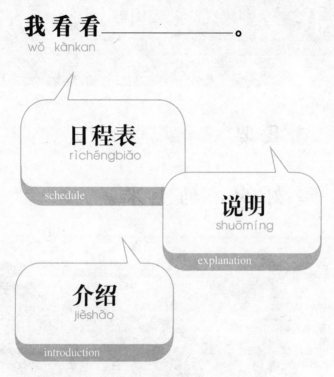

日程表
rìchéngbiǎo

schedule

说明
shuōmíng

explanation

介绍
jièshào

introduction

DO YOU KNOW?

Dishes' names on Chinese menus are full of culture. For example, Dōngpōròu (Dongpo Pork), Tàibáiyā (Taibai Duck), Bùbù Dēnggāo (Step-up Rise), Huāhǎo Yuèyuán (Perfect Conjugal Bliss), etc. Sometimes it is very difficult to understand what the dish is from the menu. If you are not clear, ask waiter to explain it to you.

86

我要一个鸡蛋炒饭。

Wǒ yào yí gè jīdàn chǎofàn.

I want fried rice with scrambled eggs.

● **我要一个鸡蛋炒饭。**
　Wǒ yào yí gè jīdàn chǎofàn.

● **好的，马上来。**
　Hǎode, mǎshàng lái.

○ I want fried rice with scrambled eggs.
● OK, it will be ready soon.

我要————————。
wǒ yào

一碗面条
yì wǎn miàntiáo

a bowel of noodles

一份三鲜汤
yí fèn sānxiāntāng

a "three delicious" soup

二两米饭
èr liǎng mǐfàn

two liang of rice

Chinese fast food has great variety, including fried rice, noodles, dumpling, etc. Most Chinese fast food is convenient and has a quick option to get with lower price and good quality. Chinese fast food is typically local produced. Trying Chinese fast food can save your time and money and help you learn more abut the local food as well.

来一瓶啤酒。
Lái yì píng píjiǔ.

A bottle of beer, please.

● 您喝点儿什么？
　Nín hē diǎnr shénme?

● 来一瓶啤酒。
　Lái yì píng píjiǔ.

○ What would you like to drink?

● A bottle of beer, please.

来 ——————。
lái

一杯茶
yì bēi chá

a cup of tea

一瓶可乐
yì píng kělè

a bottle of Coke

一杯橙汁
yì bēi chéngzhī

a glass of orange juice

DO YOU KNOW

Many kinds of drinks such as beer, Coke and juice are available in restaurants. There are many kinds of beers in China. Almost every place has its local beer. Tsingtao beer, Yanjing beer, Zhujiang beer and Xuehua beer are famous beers in China. Tea is free in some restaurants.

88

别 放 味 精。
Bié fàng wèijīng.

Don't add MSG.

● 别 放 味 精。
Bié fàng wèijīng.

● 好 的。
Hǎode.

● Don't add MSG.
● OK.

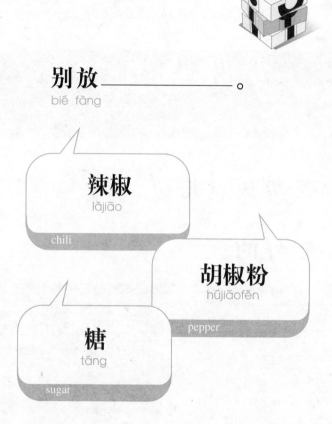

别放 ——————————— 。
bié fàng

辣椒
làjiāo
chili

胡椒粉
hújiāofěn
pepper

糖
táng
sugar

The features of Chinese food vary in different places, so it is difficult to describe it with one or two sentences. There is a saying that, "South sweet, north salty, east spicy, west sour." This means that southerners like sweet food, and northerners are fond of salty food, and people from the eastern part of the country like spicy food, while people from the western part of the country are fond of sour food.

89

少 放 点 儿 盐。

Shǎo fàng diǎnr yán.

Add only a little salt, please.

少 放 点 儿 盐。
Shǎo fàng diǎnr yán.

好 的。
Hǎode.

Add only a little salt, please.

OK.

少 放 点 儿 —————————— 。
shǎo fàng diǎnr

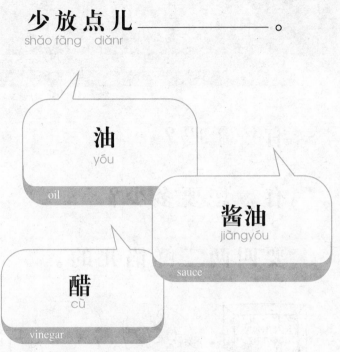

油
yóu

oil

酱油
jiàngyóu

sauce

醋
cù

vinegar

Taste is generally heavy in the north and light in the south of China. Tell the waiter or waitress your request when you order dishes.

90

有饺子吗？
Yǒu jiǎozi ma?

Do you have dumplings?

● 有饺子吗？
Yǒu jiǎozi ma?

● 有，您要多少？
Yǒu, nín yào duōshao?

● 要四两三鲜馅儿的。
Yào sì liǎng sān xiān xiànr de.

○ Do you have dumplings?
● Yes, how many do you want?
○ Four liang dumplings with "three delicious" stuffing.

有_____吗？
yǒu ma

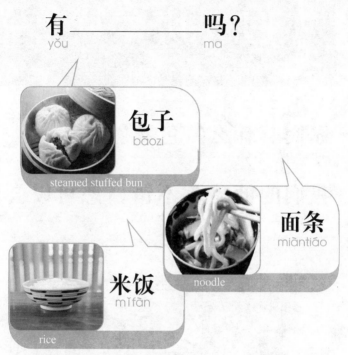

包子
bāozi
steamed stuffed bun

面条
miàntiáo
noodle

米饭
mǐfàn
rice

DO YOU KNOW?

Traditionally the staple food in northern China is flour, such as dumplings, steamed stuffed buns and noodles, while in southern China it is rice, such as cooked rice and rice noodles. However, nowadays the staple food of the north and south are interchanged and the typical staple food is not so clear now.

91

你们有什么特色菜？

Nǐmen yǒu shénme tèsècài?

What special dishes do you have?

 你们有什么特色菜？

Nǐmen yǒu shénme tèsècài?

● 我们的糖醋鱼不错，您可以尝尝。

Wǒmen de Tángcùyú búcuò, nín kěyǐ chángchang.

○ What special dishes do you have?

● Our sweat and sour fish is delicious. You can try it.

你们有什么————？
nǐmen yǒu shénme

特价菜
tèjiàcài

special dishes

凉菜
liángcài

cool dishes

主食
zhǔshí

staple food

Chinese food is full of cultural meaning and variety. The main eight Chinese cuisine styles are: Shandong cuisine, Sichuan cuisine, Guangdong cuisine, Jiangsu cuisine, Zhejiang cuisine, Fujian cuisine, Hunan cuisine and Anhui cuisine. They are different from tastes and specialties.

Dining ⊙ 就餐

92

这道菜辣不辣？
Zhè dào cài là bú là.

Is this dish spicy or not?

● 这道菜辣不辣？
Zhè dào cài là bú là?

● 有点儿辣。
Yǒudiǎnr là.

 Is this dish spicy or not?

● It is a little spicy.

这道菜————?
zhè dào cài

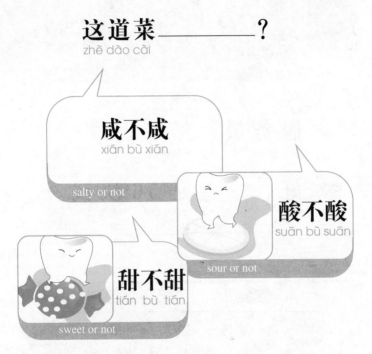

咸不咸
xián bù xián
salty or not

酸不酸
suān bù suān
sour or not

甜不甜
tián bù tián
sweet or not

Dining ◎ 就餐

185

93

服务员，结账。

Fúwùyuán, jiézhǎng

Waiter, bill please.

 服务员，结账。
Fúwùyuán, jiézhǎng.

好，一共是56块钱。
Hǎo, yígòng shì wǔshíliù kuài qián.

Waiter, bill please.

OK, totally it is 56 kuai.

服务员，————。
fúwùyuán

点菜
diǎncài

order dishes

买单
mǎidān

bill

打包
dǎbāo

pack the left food

DO YOU KNOW?

A Western breakfast is often a buffet that contains breakfast cereals, fruit, eggs, sausages, bacon, bread and toasting facilities. A Chinese breakfast will usually include a number of hot dishes such as noodles, vegetables, rice porridge and probably also fruit. A selection of steamed buns containing meat or beans will probably also be available.

我的钱包丢了！
Wǒ de qiānbāo diū le!

My wallet is lost!

● **我 的 钱包 丢 了！**
Wǒ de qiānbāo diū le!

● **别 着急，我 帮 你 找。**
Bié zhāojí, wǒ bāng nǐ zhǎo.

○ My wallet is lost!

○ Don't worry. I will help you to look for it.

我的 ———— 丢了！
wǒ de　　　　　diū le

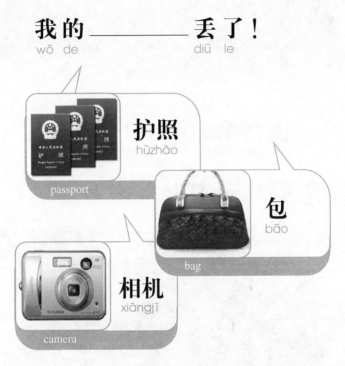

护照
hùzhào

passport

包
bāo

bag

相机
xiāngjī

camera

DO YOU KNOW

During a journey, pay attention to your bag. Don't keep your bag on back, but rather on the side of your body. Don't forget to keep an eye on your bag when you are shopping, dining, taking pictures and on the bus.

95

快 帮 我 打 110！
Kuài bāng wǒ dǎ yāoyāolíng!

Please call 110 for me!

● 快帮我打110！
Kuài bāng wǒ dǎ yāoyāolíng!

● 我马上打！
Wǒ mǎshàng dǎ!

● Please call 110 for me!
● I will call it immediately.

快帮我打——！
kuài bāng wǒ dǎ

120
yāo'èrlíng
ambulance number

122
yāo'èr'èr
traffic police number

119
yāoyāojiǔ
fire alarm number

Make several copies of your passport, traveler's checks, credit cards, itinerary, airline tickets and other travel documents. Leave one copy with a relative or friend back home and carry one copy with you. Take most of your money in traveler's checks and record the serial numbers, denominations and date and location of the issuing agency. Remove all unnecessary credit cards from your wallet. Be sure to carry your credit card and company's telephone number in case your card is lost or stolen. Always report losses immediately.

96

快叫警察！
Kuài jiāo jǐngchá!

Please call the police!

 快叫警察！
Kuài jiāo jǐngchá!

 **好。**
Hǎo.

Please call the police!

OK.

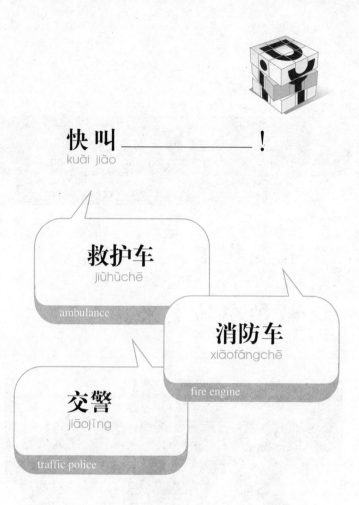

快叫 —————!
kuài jiào

救护车
jiǔhùchē
ambulance

消防车
xiāofángchē
fire engine

交警
jiāojǐng
traffic police

When traveling to a country far from your home, one should always expect the unexpected. It is part of the nature of travel. Travel insurance always helps. With a small premium, it covers trip cancellation, luggage damage or loss, accidents on the trip, etc. Check with your travel agent for more detailed programs.

97

我受伤了！
Wǒ shòushāng le!

I am injured!

我受伤了！
Wǒ shòushāng le!

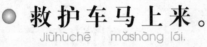

救护车马上来。
Jiùhùchē mǎshàng lái.

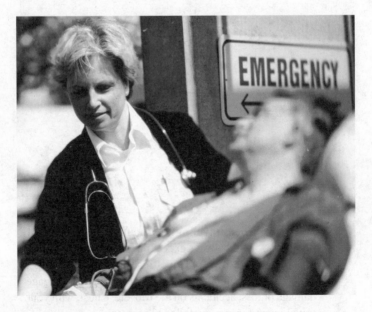

I am injured!

The ambulance will come soon.

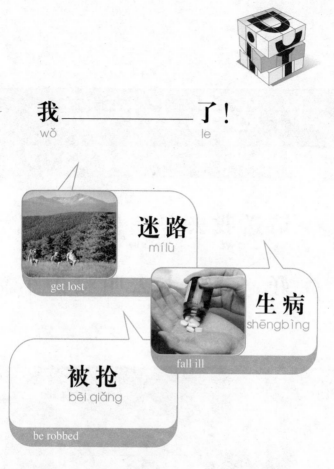

我 ————— 了!
wǒ   le

迷路
mílù
get lost

生病
shēngbìng
fall ill

被抢
bèi qiǎng
be robbed

Useful Travel Medicines

止泻丸	zhǐxièwán	pills to stop diarrhea
止痛药	zhǐtòngyào	anodyne
感冒药	gǎnmàoyào	cold medicine
晕车药	yūnchēyào	medicine for carsickness
防晒乳液	fángshài rǔyè	sun block
创可贴	chuāngkětiē	brand adhesive bandages

98

请送我去医院！
Qǐng sòng wǒ qù yīyuàn!

Please take me to the hospital!

● **请送我去医院！**
Qǐng sòng wǒ qù yīyuàn!

● **好，我马上去叫救护车。**
Hǎo, wǒ mǎshàng qù jiào jiùhùchē.

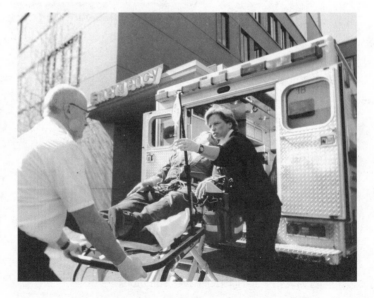

○ Please take me to the hospital!
● OK, I will call ambulance immediately.

请送我去———！
qǐng sòng wǒ qù

警察局
jǐngchájú
police station

大使馆
dàshǐguǎn
embassy

学校
xuéxiào
school

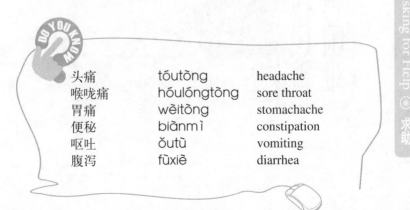

头痛	tóutòng	headache
喉咙痛	hóulóngtòng	sore throat
胃痛	wèitòng	stomachache
便秘	biànmì	constipation
呕吐	ǒutù	vomiting
腹泻	fùxiè	diarrhea

99

请帮我给大使馆打电话。

Qǐng bāng wǒ gěi dàshǐguǎn dǎ diànhuà.

Please call the embassy for me.

🔵 **请帮我给大使馆打电话。**

Qǐng bāng wǒ gěi dàshǐguǎn dǎ diànhuà.

🔵 **电话号码是多少？**

Diànhuà hàomǎ shì duōshao?

🔵 Please call the embassy for me.

🔵 What is the telephone number?

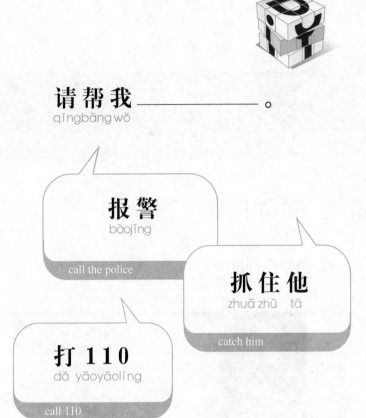

请帮我 ————————。
qǐng bāng wǒ

报警
bàojǐng

call the police

抓住他
zhuā zhù tā

catch him

打 110
dǎ yāoyāolíng

call 110

Travelers are advised to check with their doctors before visiting China. A Health Declaration form must be completed upon arrival. No immunizations are required for short-term travelers, unless you are coming from or through a yellow fever infected area. You should also bring any special health remedies or medications you require, as well as over-the-counter items. Travel to high-altitude areas such as Tibet is not recommended for those with pulmonary or heart problems.

100

救命！
Jiùmìng!

Help!

救命！
Jiùmìng!

怎么啦？
Zěnme la?

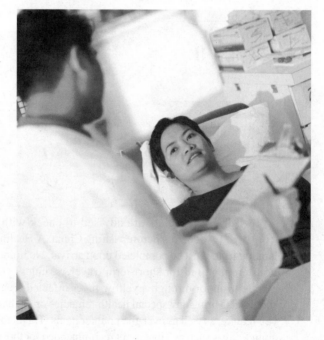

Help!

What's the matter?

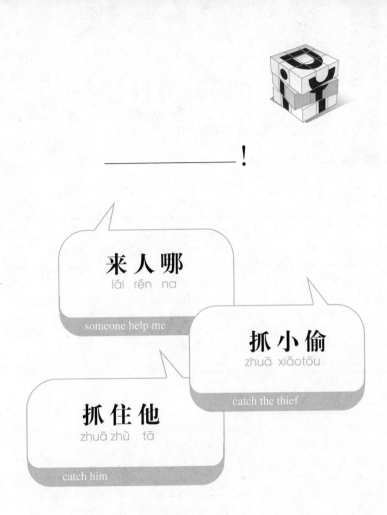

_____!

来人哪
lái rén na

someone help me

抓小偷
zhuā xiǎotōu

catch the thief

抓住他
zhuā zhù tā

catch him

It's very important to learn how to ask for help in an emergency during your journey. If something unexpected happens, try to ask for help. Do not face it alone.

中国的节日
Zhōngguó de　　jiérì
Chinese Holidays

元旦 Yuándàn	New Year's Day (January 1st)
春节 Chūnjié	Spring Festival (the 1st day of the 1st lunar month)
元宵节 Yuánxiāojié	Lantern Festival (the 15th day of the 1st lunar month)
国际妇女节 Gúojì Fùnǚjié	International Women's Day (March 8th)
植树节 Zhíshùjié	Arbor Day (March 12th)
国际消费者 Guójì Xiāofèizhě **权益日** Quányìrì	World Consumer Right Day (March 15th)
清明节 Qīngmíngjié	Tomb-Sweeping Day (April 5th)
国际劳动节 Guójì Láodòngjié	International Labor Day (May 1st)
青年节 Qīngniánjié	Chinese Youth Day (May 4th)

端午节 Duānwǔjié	Dragon Boat Festival (the 5th day of the 5th lunar month)
国际儿童节 Guójì Értóngjié	International Children's Day (June 1st)
中国共产党 Zhōngguó Gòngchǎndǎng **诞生纪念日** Dànshēng Jìniànrì	Anniversary of the Founding of the Chinese Communist Party (July 1st)
七夕情人节 Qīxī Qíngrénjié	Double Seventh Festival/ Chinese Valentine's Day (the 7th day of the 7th lunar month)
建军节 Jiànjūnjié	Army Day (August 1st)
教师节 Jiàoshījié	Teacher's Day (September 10th)
国庆节 Guóqìngjié	National Day (October 1st)
中秋节 Zhōngqiūjié	Mid-Autumn Festival (the 15th day of the 8th lunar month)
重阳节 Chóngyángjié	Double Ninth Festival (the 9th day of the 9th lunar month)

中国世界遗产列表
Zhōngguó shìjiè yíchǎn lièbiǎo
China World Heritage

长城 Chángchéng	The Great Wall
明清故宫 Míng Qīng Gùgōng	Imperial Palaces of the Ming and Qing Dynasties
莫高窟 Mōgāokū	Mogao Caves
秦始皇陵及兵马俑坑 Qínshǐhuánglíng jí Bīngmǎyǒngkēng	Mausoleum of the First Qin Emperor and Terracotta Warriors
周口店北京人遗址 Zhōukǒudiàn Běijīngrén Yízhǐ	Peking Man Site at Zhoukoudian
泰山 Tàishān	Mount Taishan
黄山 Huángshān	Mount Huangshan
九寨沟风景名胜区 Jiǔzhàigōu Fēngjǐng Míngshèngqū	Jiuzhaigou Valley Scenic and Historic Interest Area
黄龙风景名胜区 Huánglóng Fēngjǐng Míngshèngqū	Huanglong Scenic and Historic Interest Area
武陵源风景名胜区 Wǔlíngyuán Fēngjǐng Míngshèngqū	Wulingyuan Scenic and Historic Interest Area

承德避暑山庄及其周围寺庙 Chéngdé Bìshǔshānzhuāng jíqí Zhōuwéi Sìmiào	Mountain Restort and its Outlying Temples
曲阜孔庙、孔林、孔府 Qūfù Kǒngmiào Kǒnglín Kǒngfǔ	Temple and Cemetery of Confucius and the Kong Family Mansion in Qufu
布达拉宫 Bùdálāgōng	Historic Ensemble of the Potala Palace
武当山古建筑群 Wǔdāngshān Gǔjiànzhùqún	Ancient Building Complex in the Wudang Mountains
峨眉山－乐山大佛 Éméishān Lèshān Dàfó	Mount Emei Senic Area including Leshan Giant Buddha Scenic Area
庐山国家公园 Lúshān Guójiā Gōngyuán	Lushan National Park
丽江古城 Lìjiāng Gǔchéng	Old Town of Lijiang
平遥古城 Píngyáo Gǔchéng	Ancient City of Pingyao
苏州古典园林 Sūzhōu Gǔdiǎn Yuánlín	Classical Gardens of Suzhou
颐和园 Yíhéyuán	Summer Palace, an Imperial Garden in Beijing
天坛 Tiāntán	Temple of Heaven
武夷山 Wǔyíshān	Mount Wuyi

大足石刻 Dàzú Shíkè	Dazu Rock Carvings
青城山和都江堰 Qīngchéngshān hé Dūjiāngyàn **水利工程** Shuǐlì Gōngchéng	Mount Qingcheng and the Dujiangyan Irrigation System
皖南古村落——西递、宏村 Wǎnnán Gǔcūnluò Xīdì Hóngcūn	Ancient Villages in Southern Anhui–Xidi and Hongcun
龙门石窟 Lóngmén Shíkū	Longmen Grottoes
明清皇家陵寝 Míng Qīng Huángjiā Língqǐn	Imperial Tombs of the Ming and Qing Dynasties
云岗石窟 Yúngǎng Shíkū	Yungang Grottoes
云南三江并流保护区 Yúnnán Sānjiāng Bìngliú Bǎohùqū	Three Parallel Rivers of Yunnan Protected Areas
中国高句丽王城、王陵 Zhōngguó Gāogōulì Wángchéng Wánglíng **及贵族墓葬** jí Guìzú Mùzàng	Capital Cities and Tombs of the Ancient Koguryo Kingdom
澳门历史城区 Àomén Lìshǐ Chéngqū	Historic Center of Macao
四川大熊猫栖息地 Sìchuān Dàxióngmāo Qīxīdì	Sichuan Giant Panda Sanctuaries
殷墟 Yīnxū	Yin Xu

常用计量单位换算表 Conversion Tables

长度 Length

1英里 [mile] =1.6093千米 [kilometer]
1千米 [kilometer] =2市里 [li] =0.621英里 [mile]
1英尺 [foot] =0.305米 [meter] =0.914市尺 [chi]
1米 [meter] =3市尺 [chi] = 3.281英尺 [feet]

重量 Weight

1千克(公斤) [kilogram] =2市斤 [jin] =2.205磅 [pound]
1市斤 [jin] =0.5千克 [kilogram] =1.102磅 [pound]
1磅 [pound] =0.454千克(公斤) [kilogram] =0.907市斤 [jin]

容积 Capacity

1升 [liter] =0.22加仑 [gallon]
1加仑 [gallon] =4.546升 [liter]

紧急电话号码 Emergency Phone Numbers

报警电话 police call 110
火警电话 fire alarm 119
急救中心 first aid 120
交通事故 traffic accident 122

郑 重 声 明

高等教育出版社依法对本书享有专有出版权。任何未经许可的复制、销售行为均违反《中华人民共和国著作权法》，其行为人将承担相应的民事责任和行政责任，构成犯罪的，将被依法追究刑事责任。为了维护市场秩序，保护读者的合法权益，避免读者误用盗版书造成不良后果，我社将配合行政执法部门和司法机关对违法犯罪的单位和个人给予严厉打击。社会各界人士如发现上述侵权行为，希望及时举报，本社将奖励举报有功人员。

反盗版举报电话：(010) 58581897/58581896/58581879

传　真：(010) 82086060

E - mail：dd@hep.com.cn

通信地址：北京市西城区德外大街 4 号

　　　　　　高等教育出版社打击盗版办公室

邮　编：100120

购书请拨打电话：(010)58581118

图书在版编目（CIP）数据

体验汉语100句. 旅游类:英语版 / 张如梅编. —北京：
高等教育出版社,2007.3(2009 重印)
ISBN 978 - 7 - 04 - 020315 - 8

Ⅰ.体… Ⅱ.张… Ⅲ.汉语 - 口语 - 对外汉语教学 - 自
学参考资料 Ⅳ.H195.4

中国版本图书馆 CIP 数据核字（2007）第 035331 号

出版发行	高等教育出版社		购书热线	010 - 58581118	
社　　址	北京市西城区德外大街 4 号		免费咨询	800 - 810 - 0598	
邮政编码	100120		网　　址	http://www.hep.edu.cn	
总　　机	010 - 58581000			http://www.hep.com.cn	
			网上订购	http://www.landraco.com	
				http://www.landraco.com.cn	
经　　销	蓝色畅想图书发行有限公司		畅想教育	http://www.widedu.com	
印　　刷	高等教育出版社印刷厂				
开　　本	889×1194　1/32				
印　　张	6.75		版　　次	2007 年 3 月第 1 版	
字　　数	160 000		印　　次	2009 年 12 月第 3 次	

如有印装等质量问题,请到所购图书销售部门调换。ISBN 978 - 7 - 04 - 020315 - 8
02800